It is important where a photo starts and ends, but the most important would be "why?". What makes me trigger the shutter? The answer would be according to the complexity of each photographer. Life experiences, culture and many other aspects are what develop the vision of each of us. No matter how much I try to capture and transmit, every time it depends on the person watching. Every photo has as many stories as the people who look at.

January 15, 2020 is the day when all the following photos were taken. A foggy day, very much to my liking because I love fog. I was inspired by what I found around me and I let my intuition pass through the filters of my own vision. A lot is happening around us and we just have to go outside and feel as if the universal consciousness asks us to photograph its manifestation through the worldly.

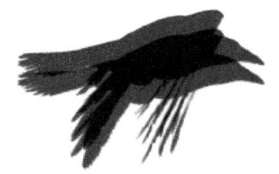

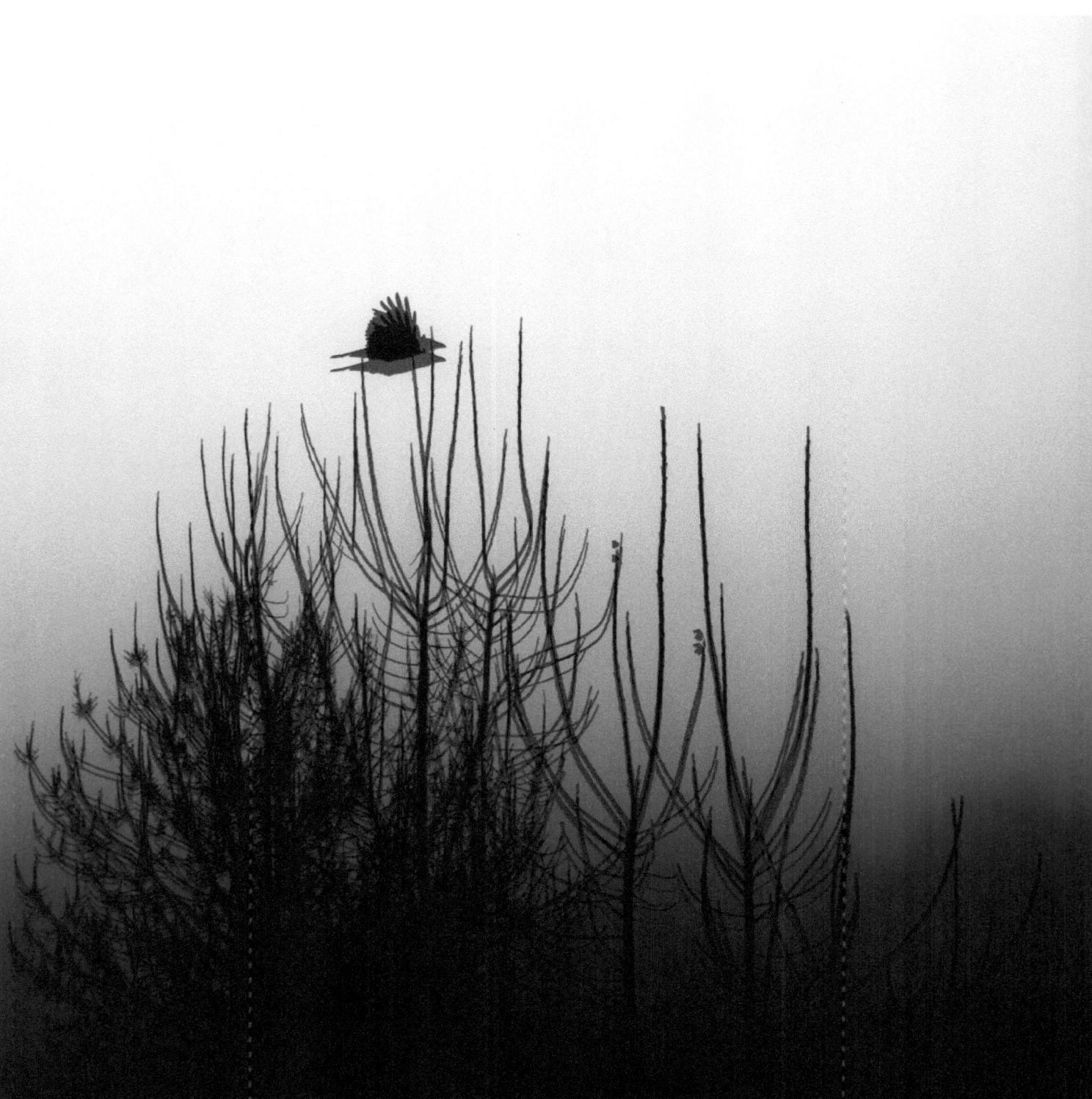

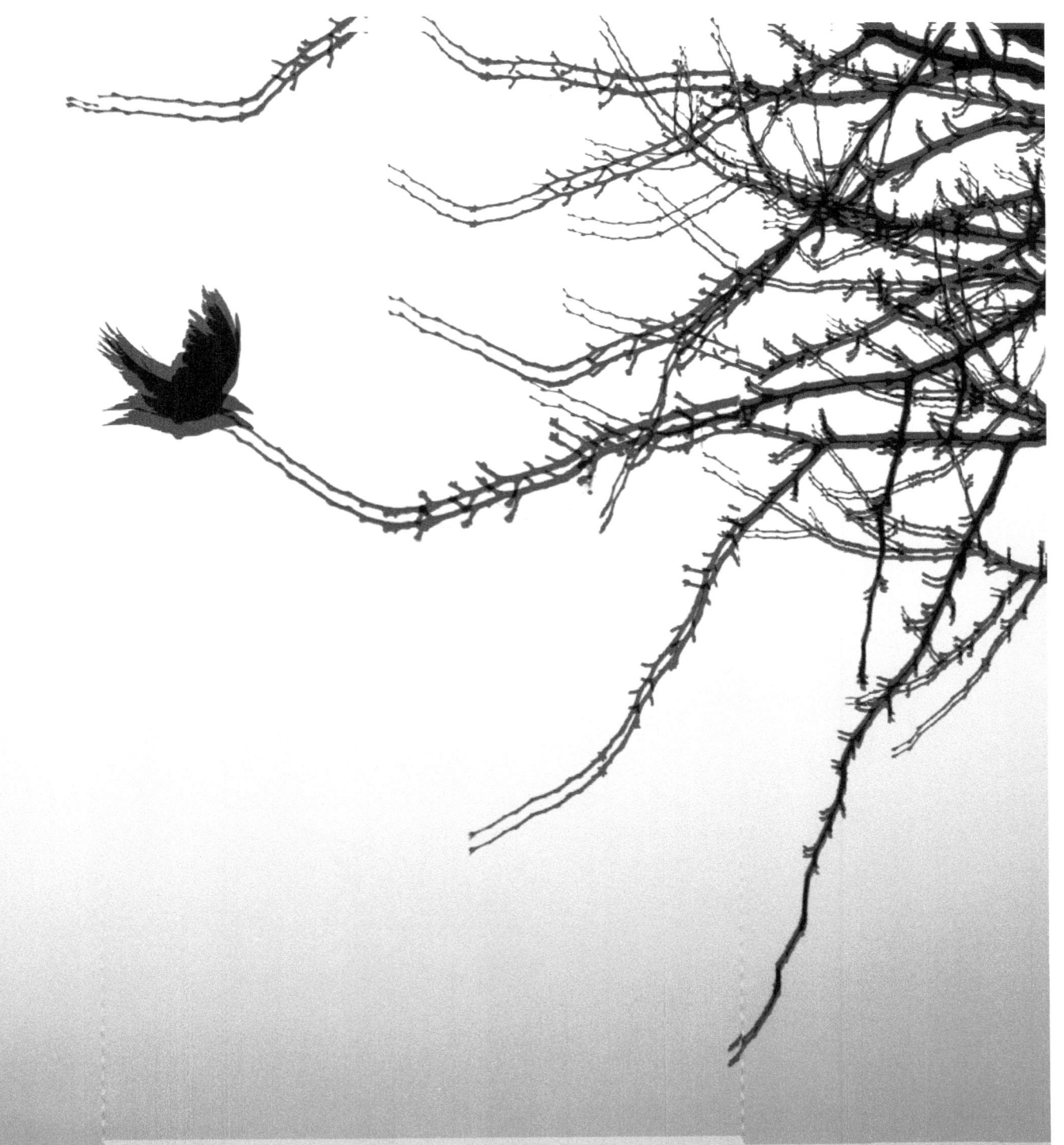

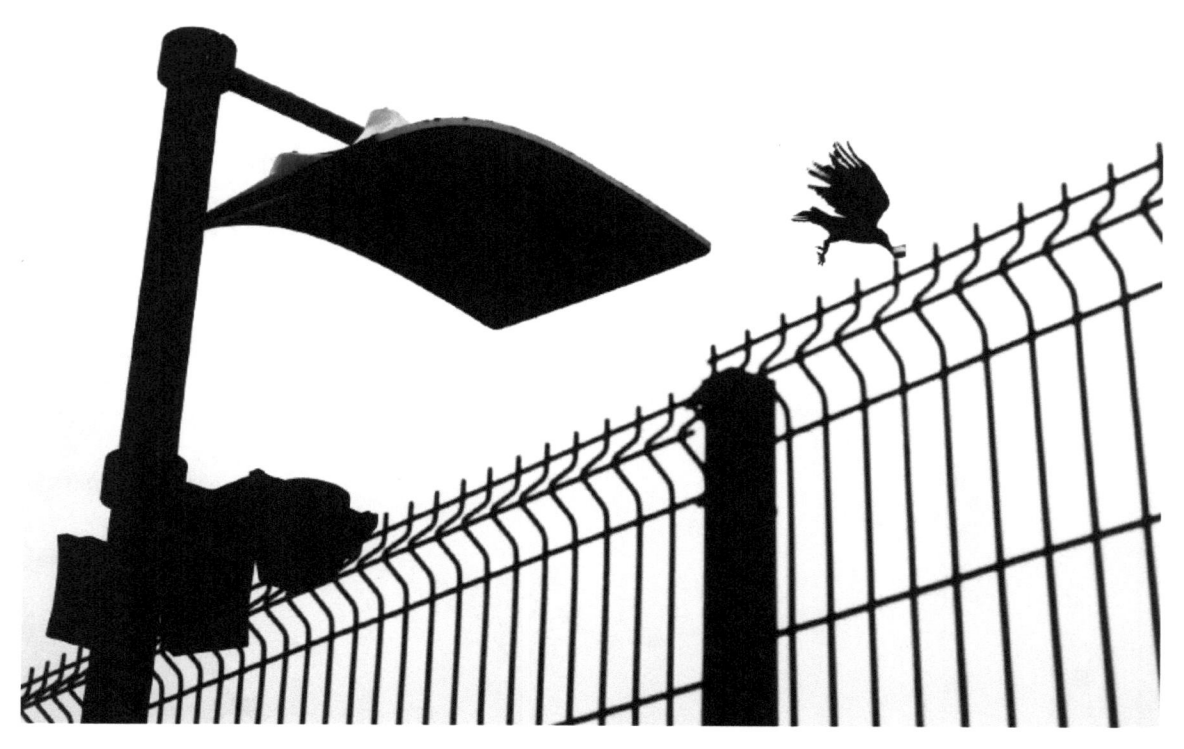
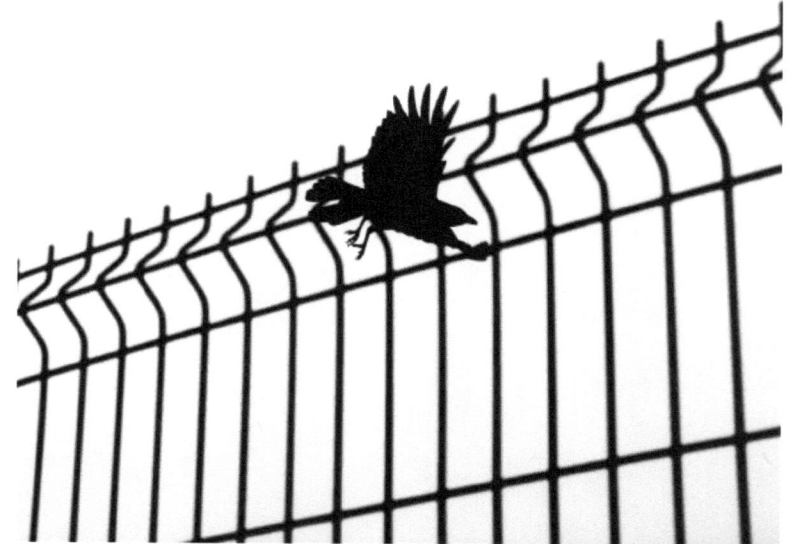

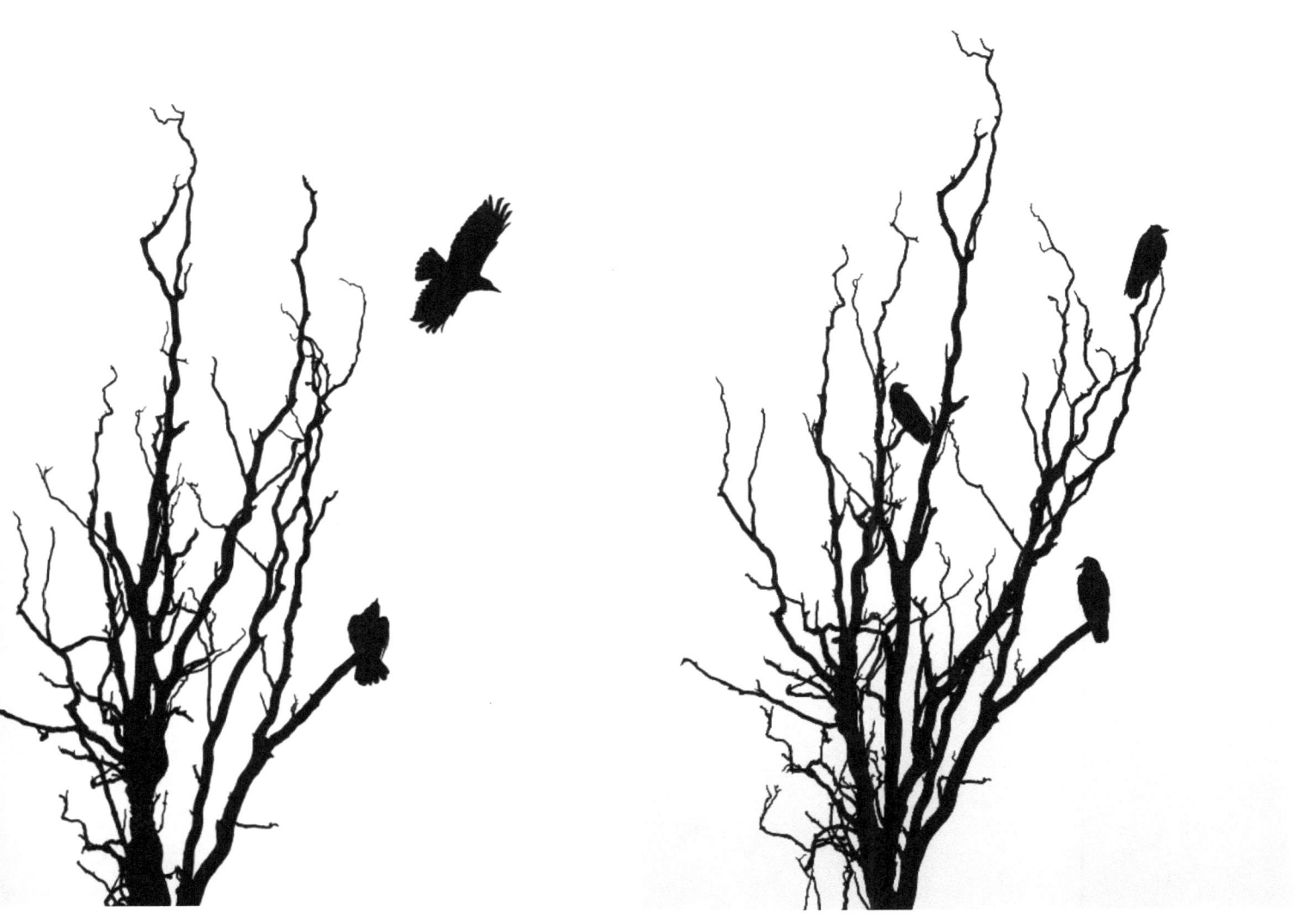

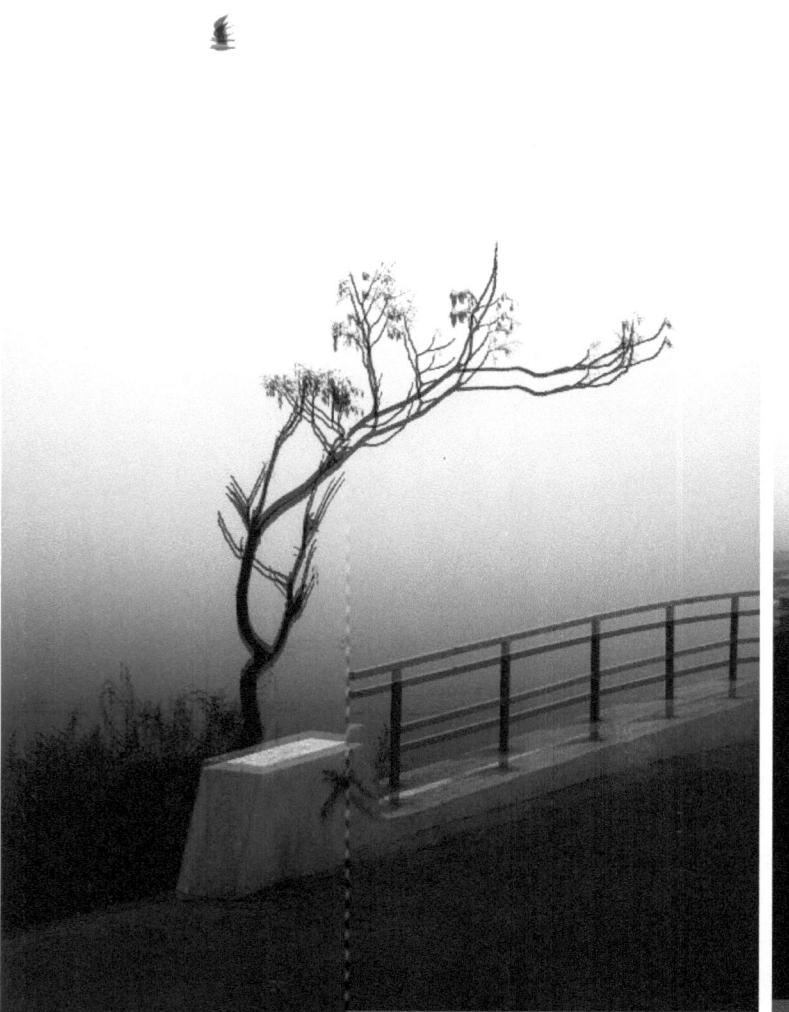

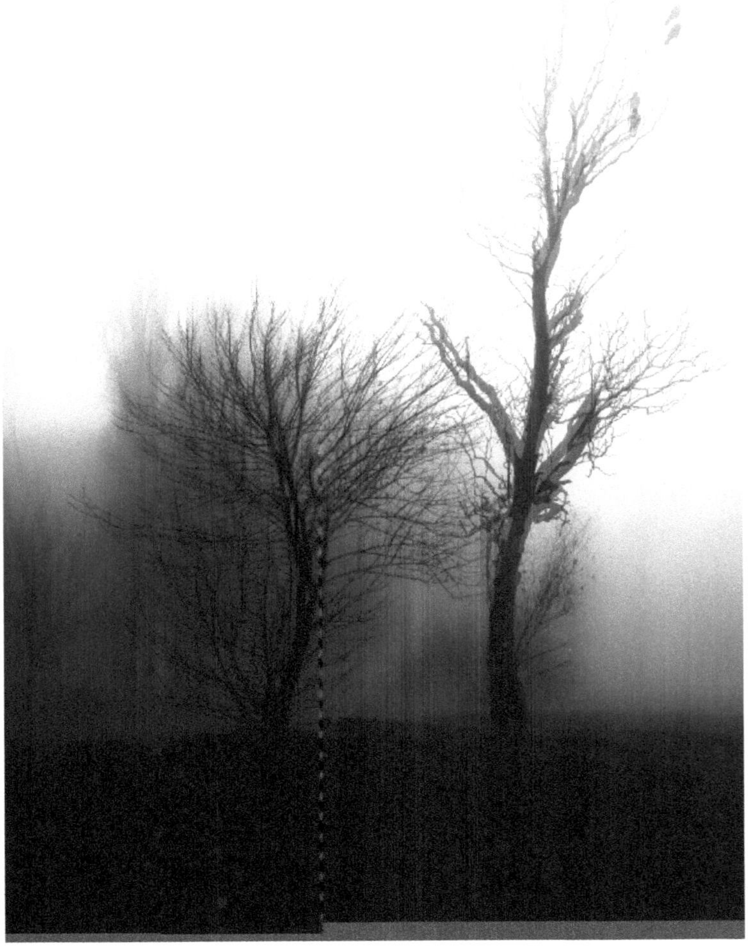

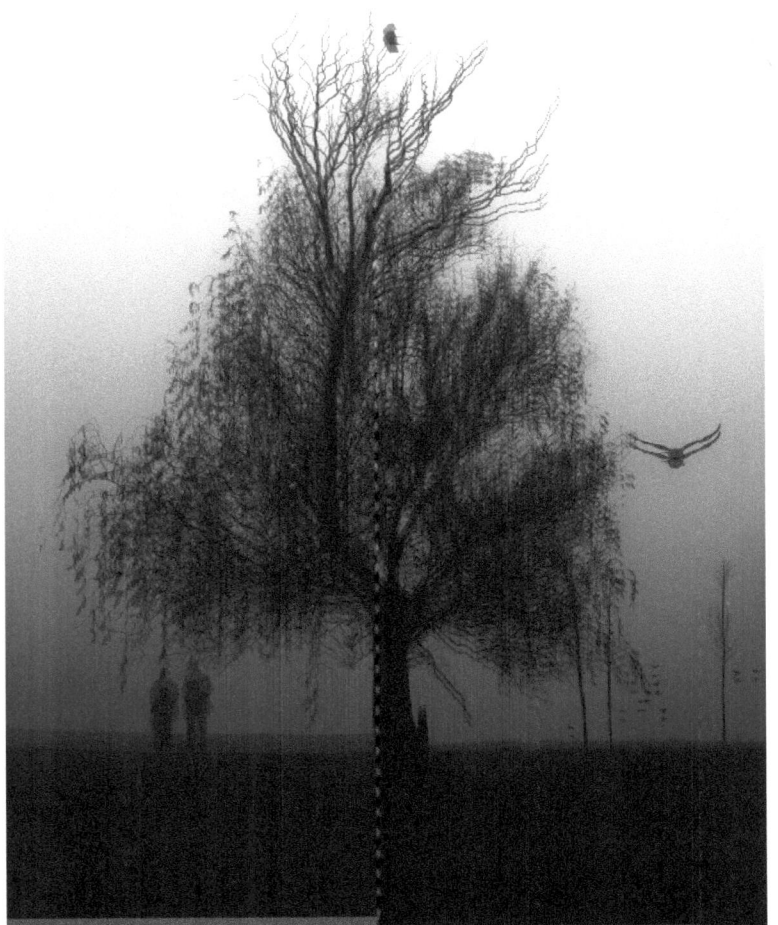

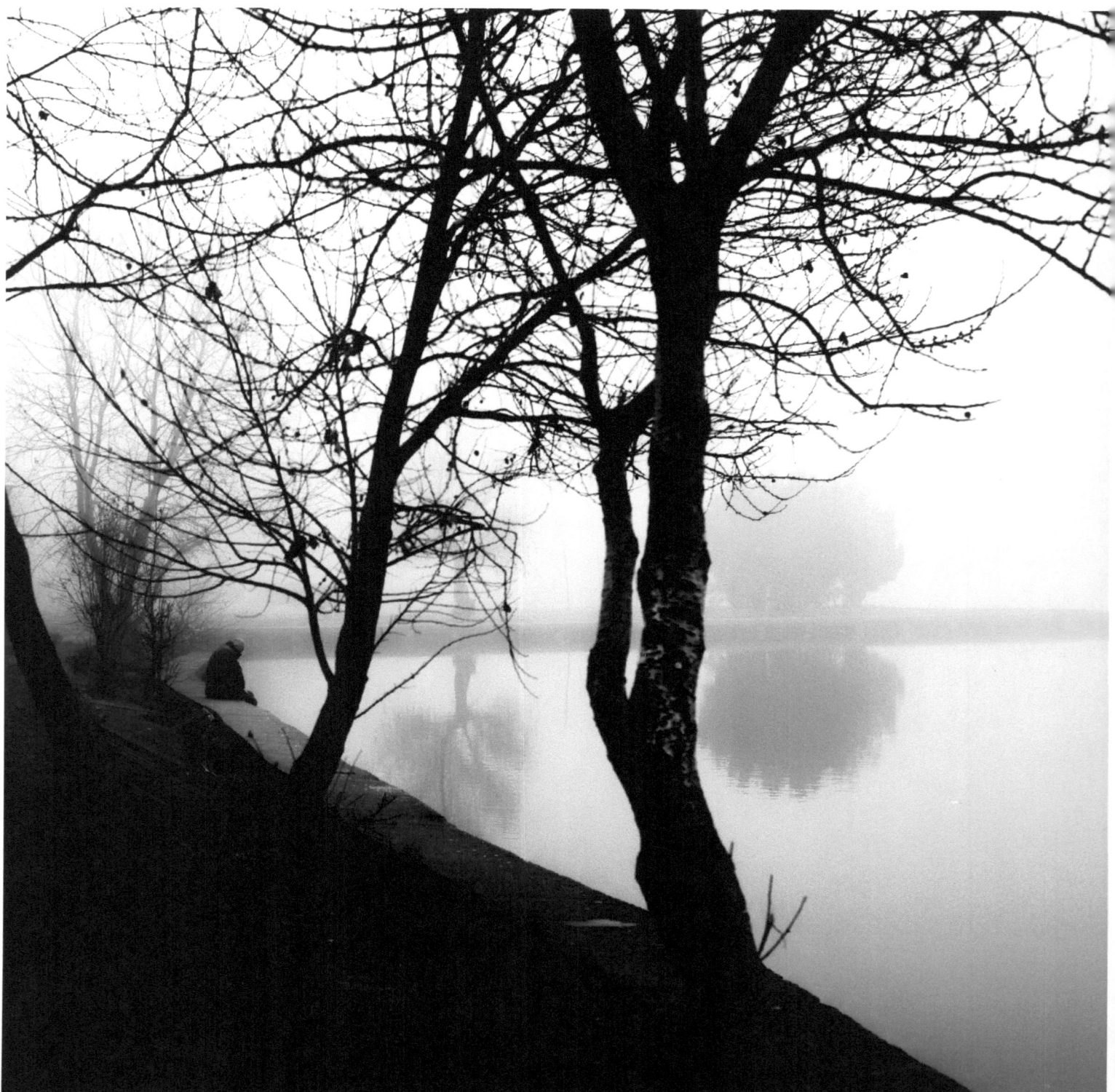

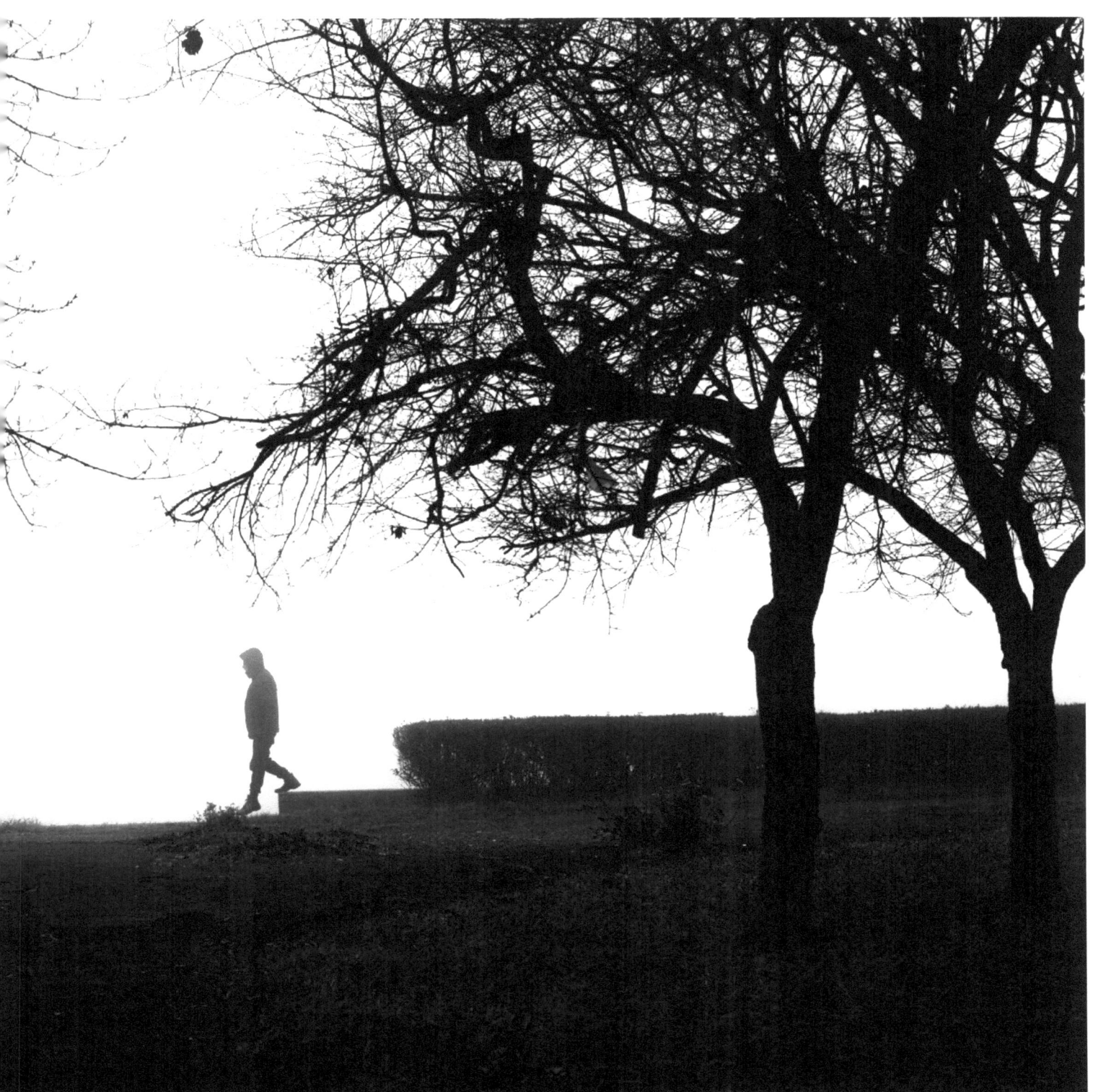

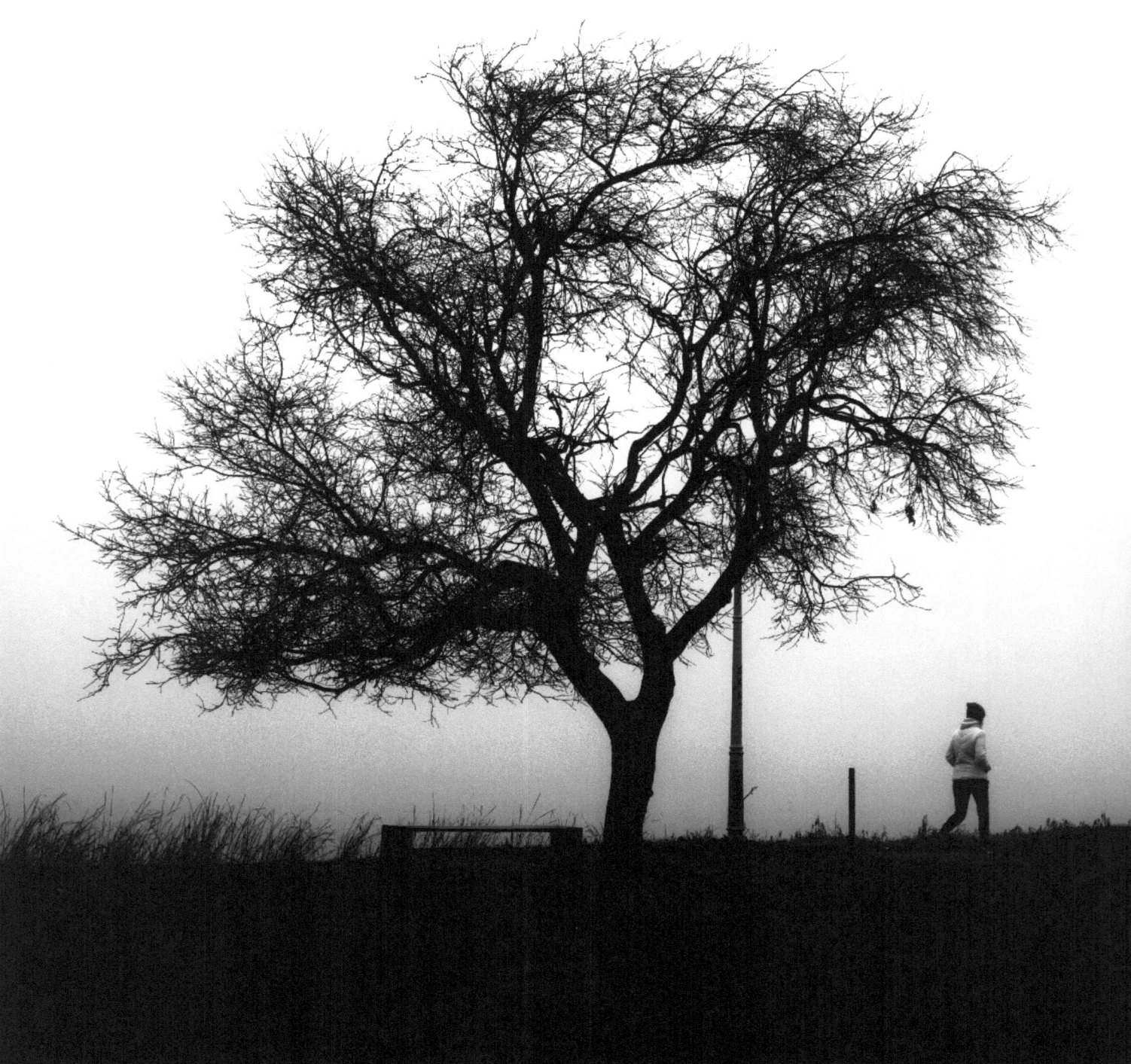

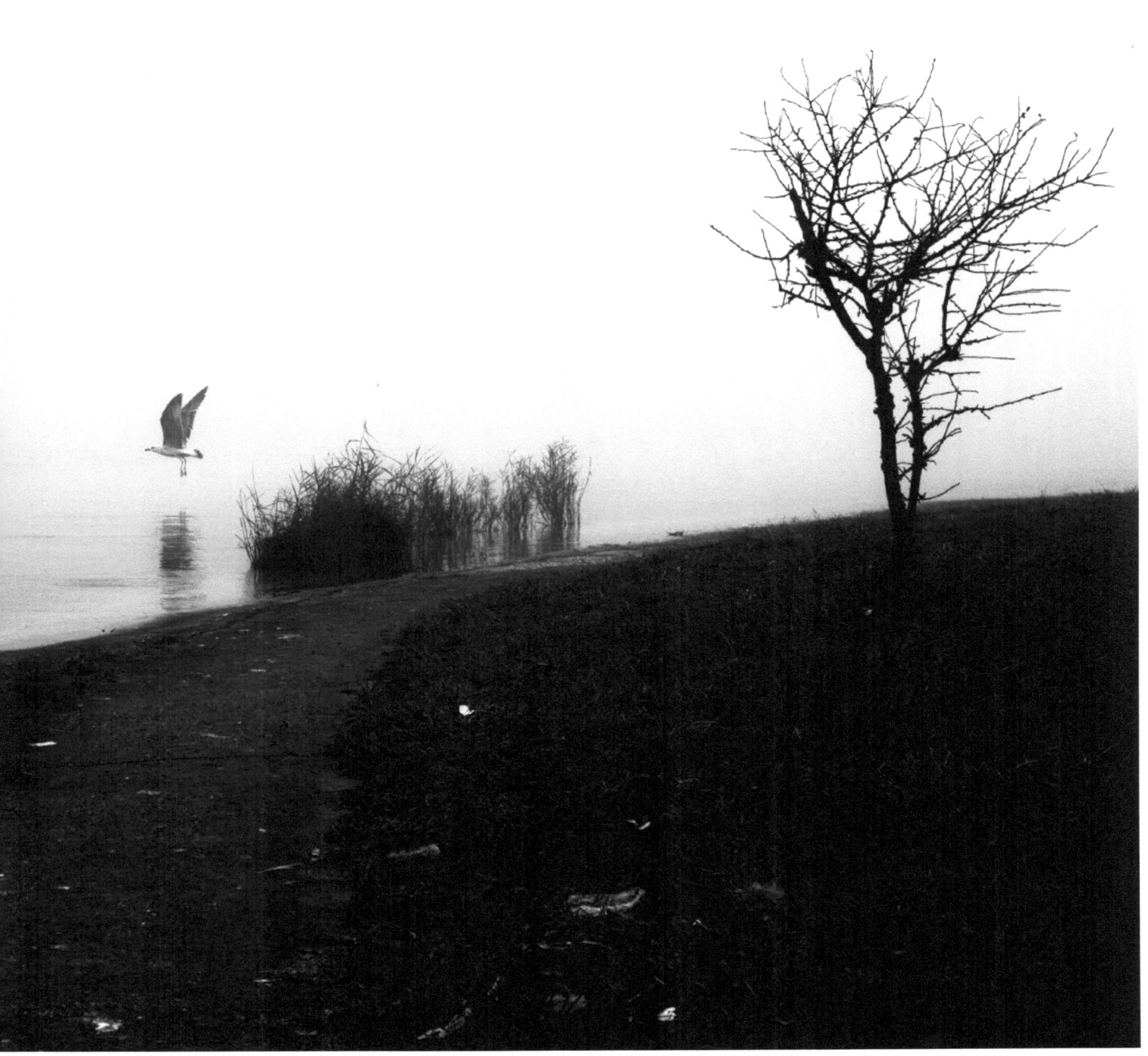

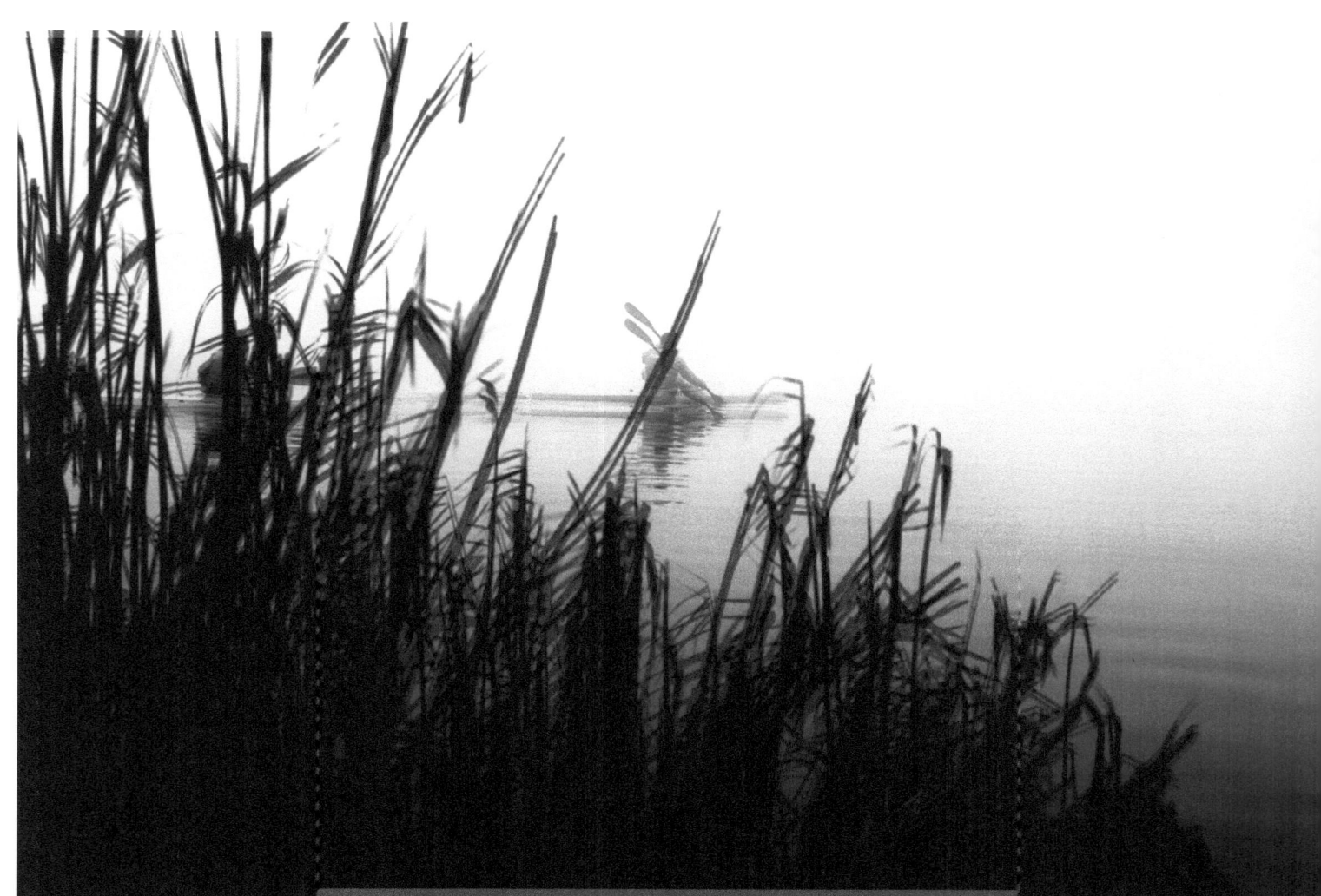

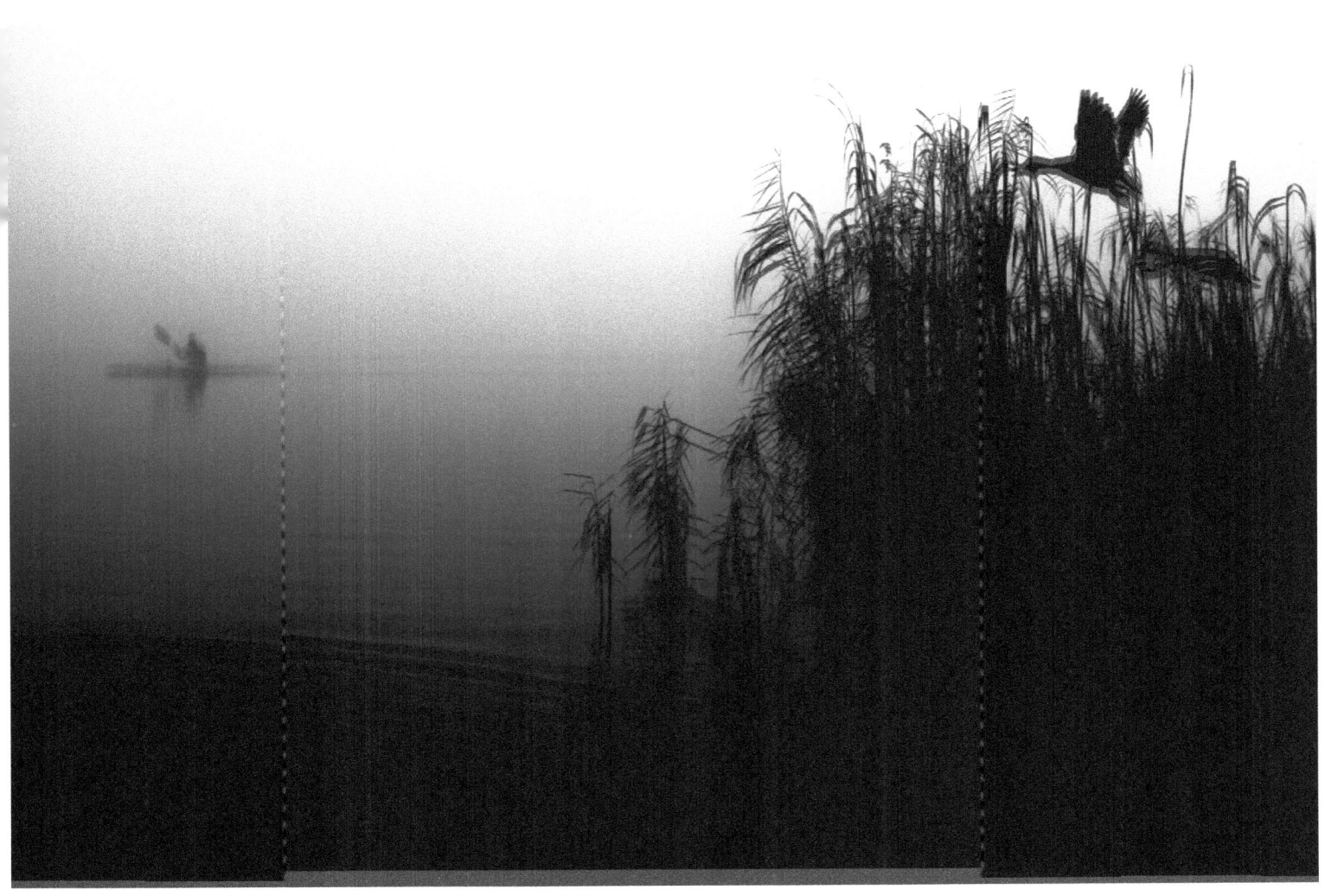

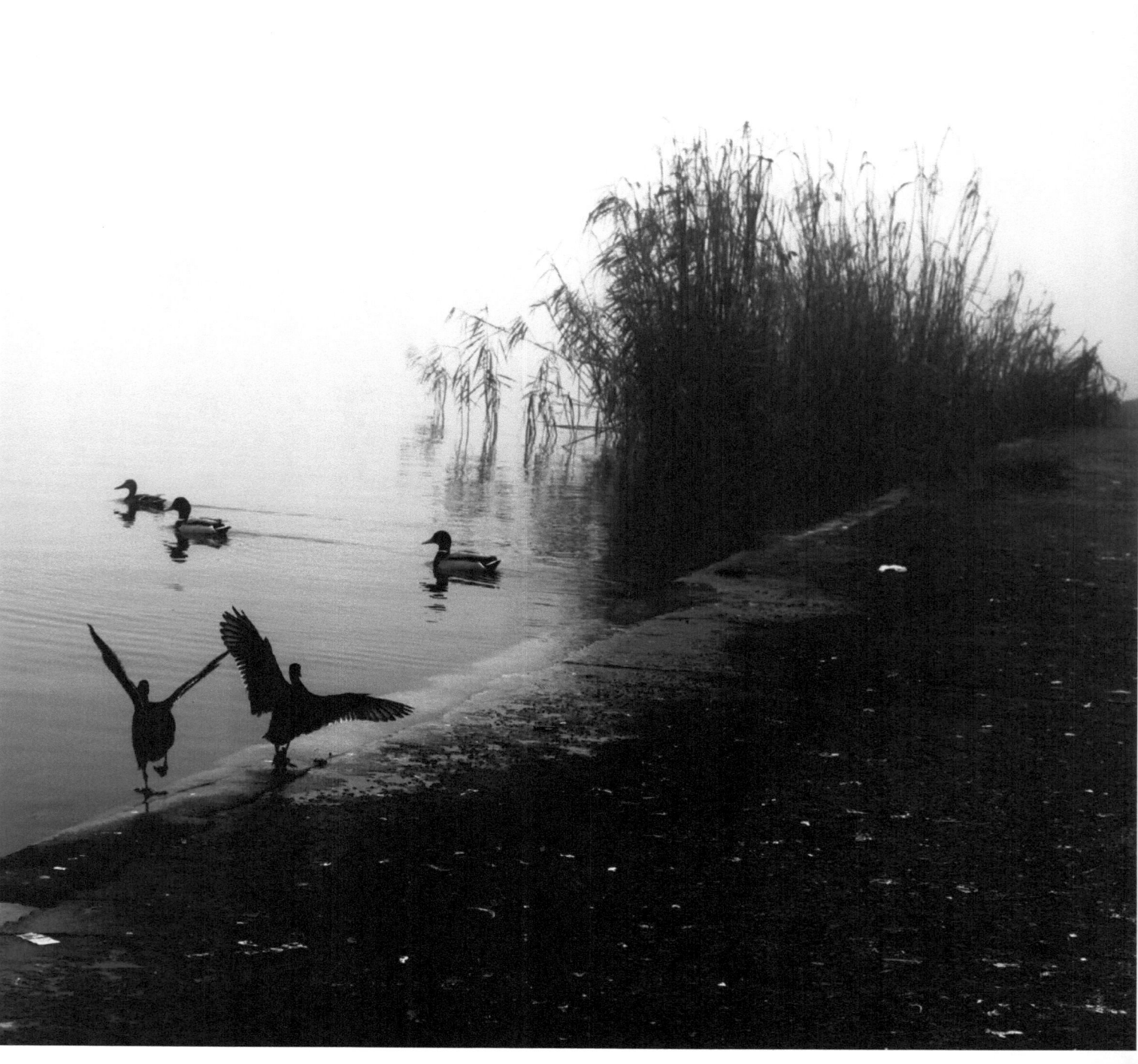

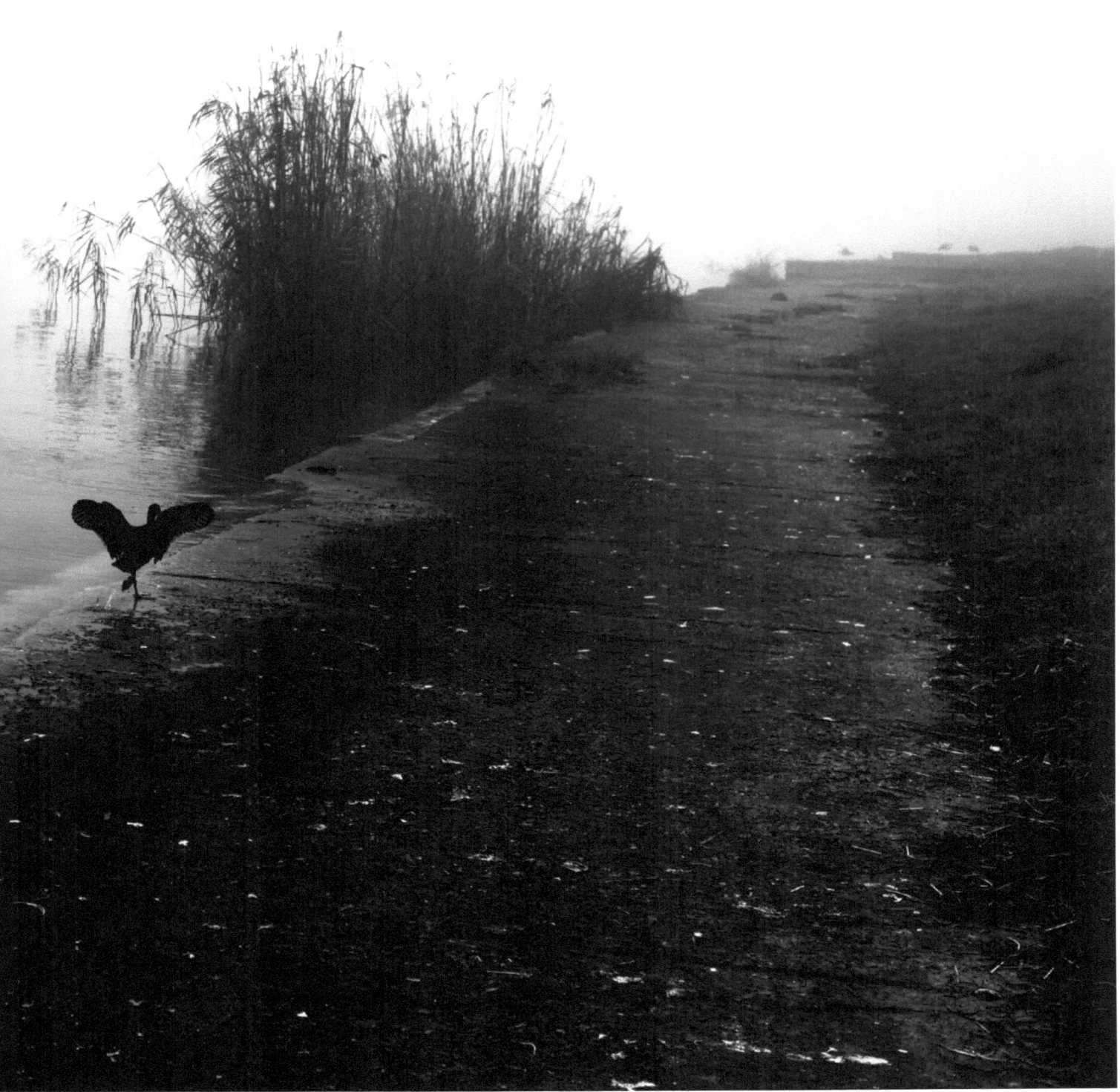

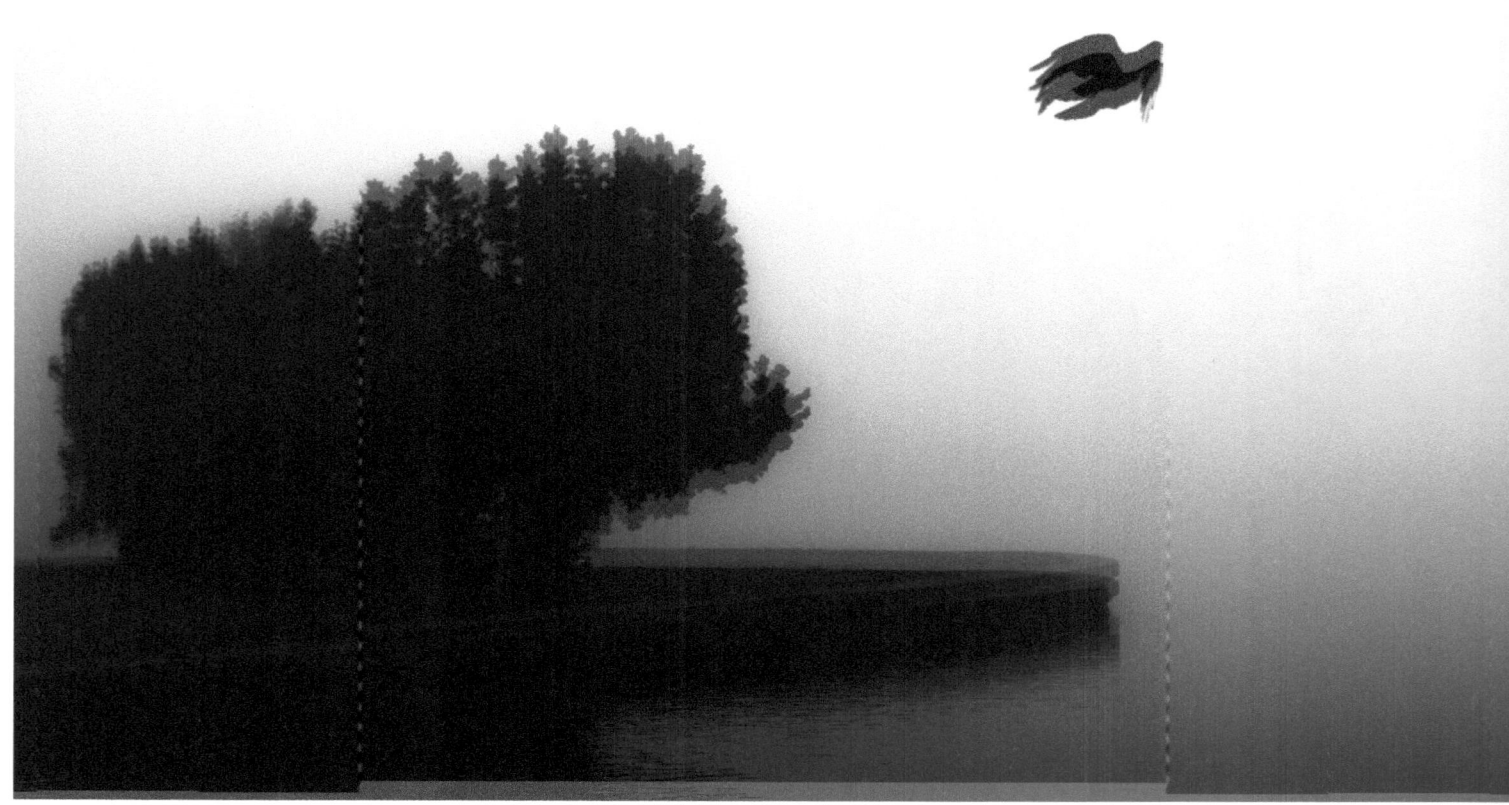

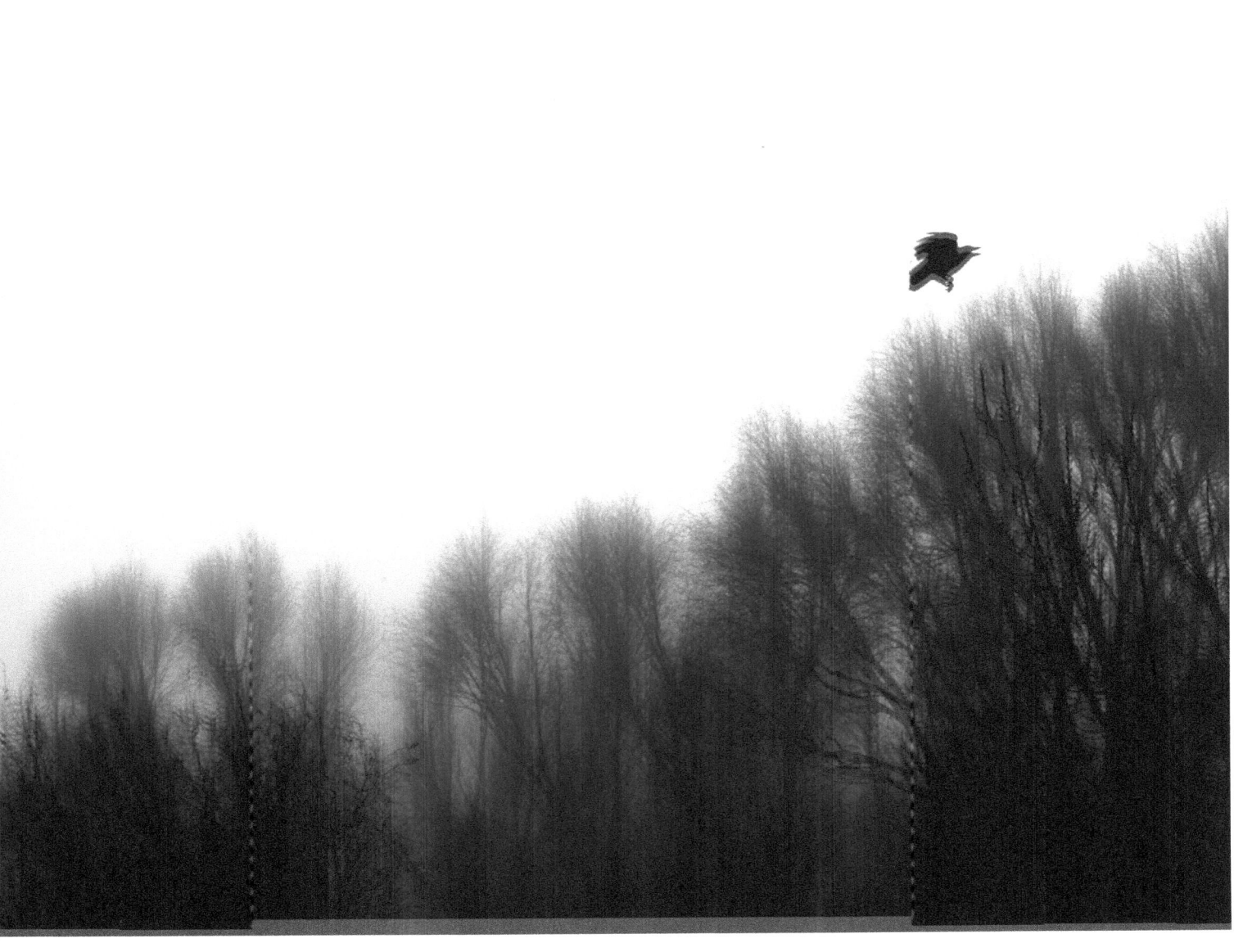

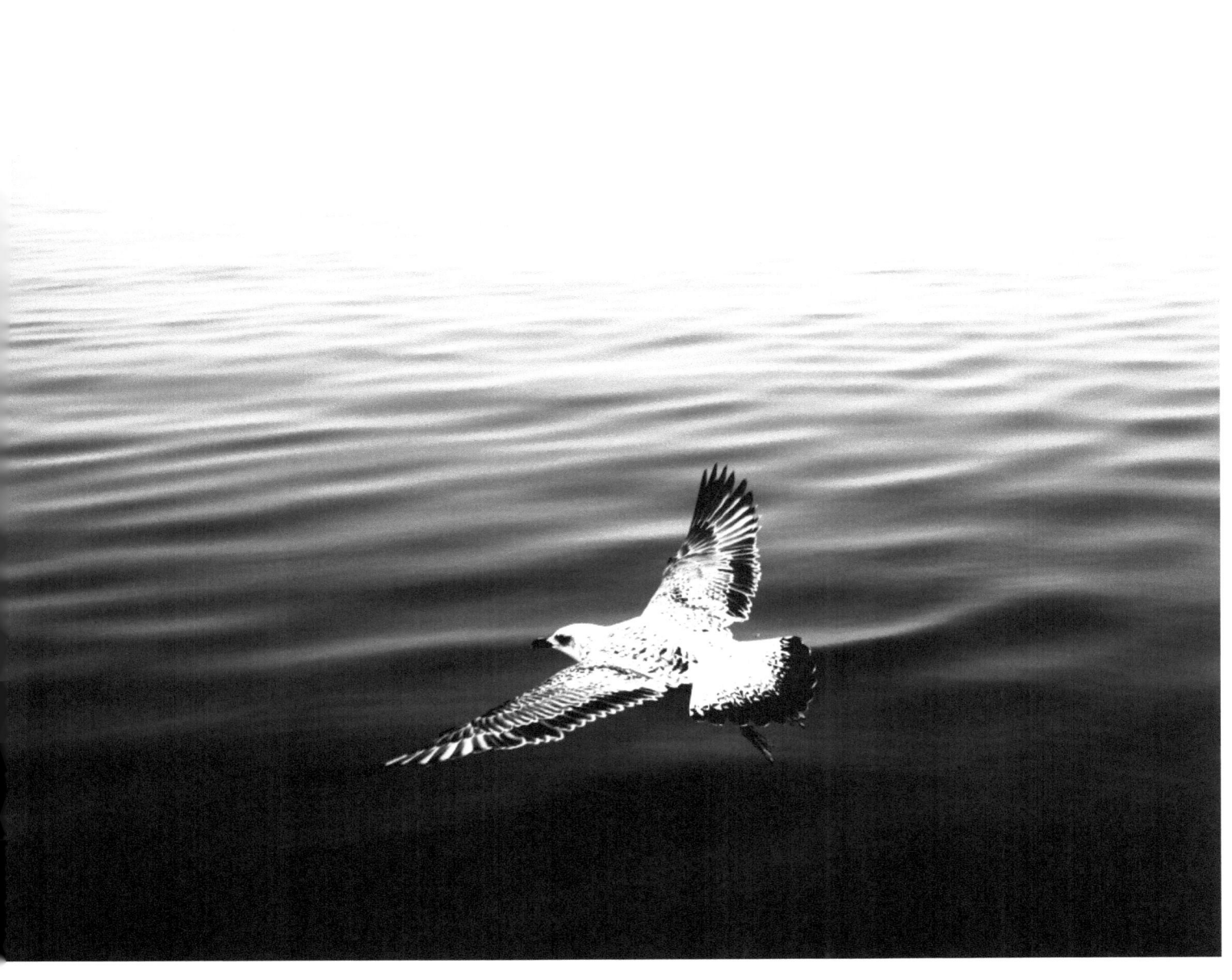

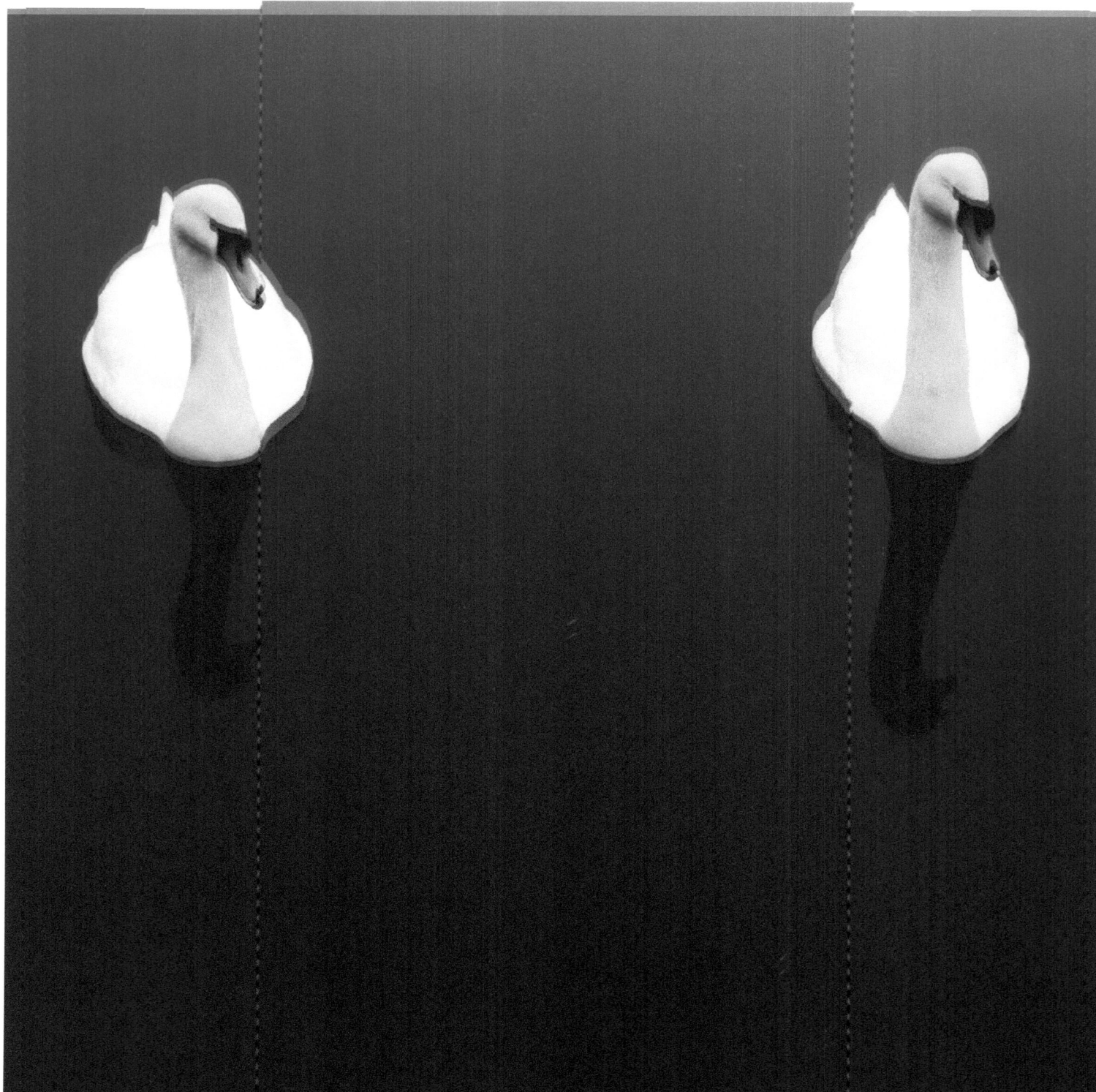

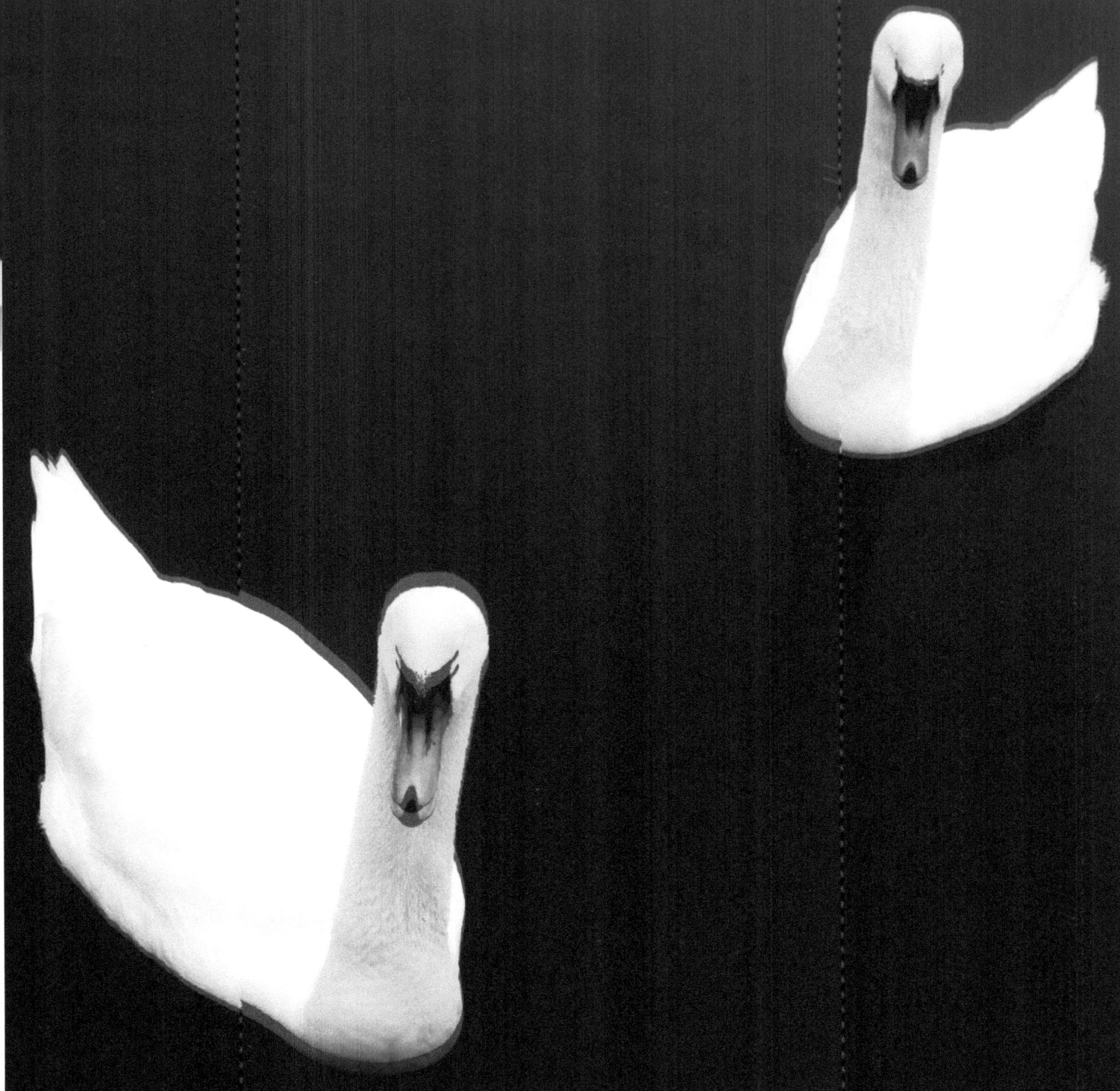

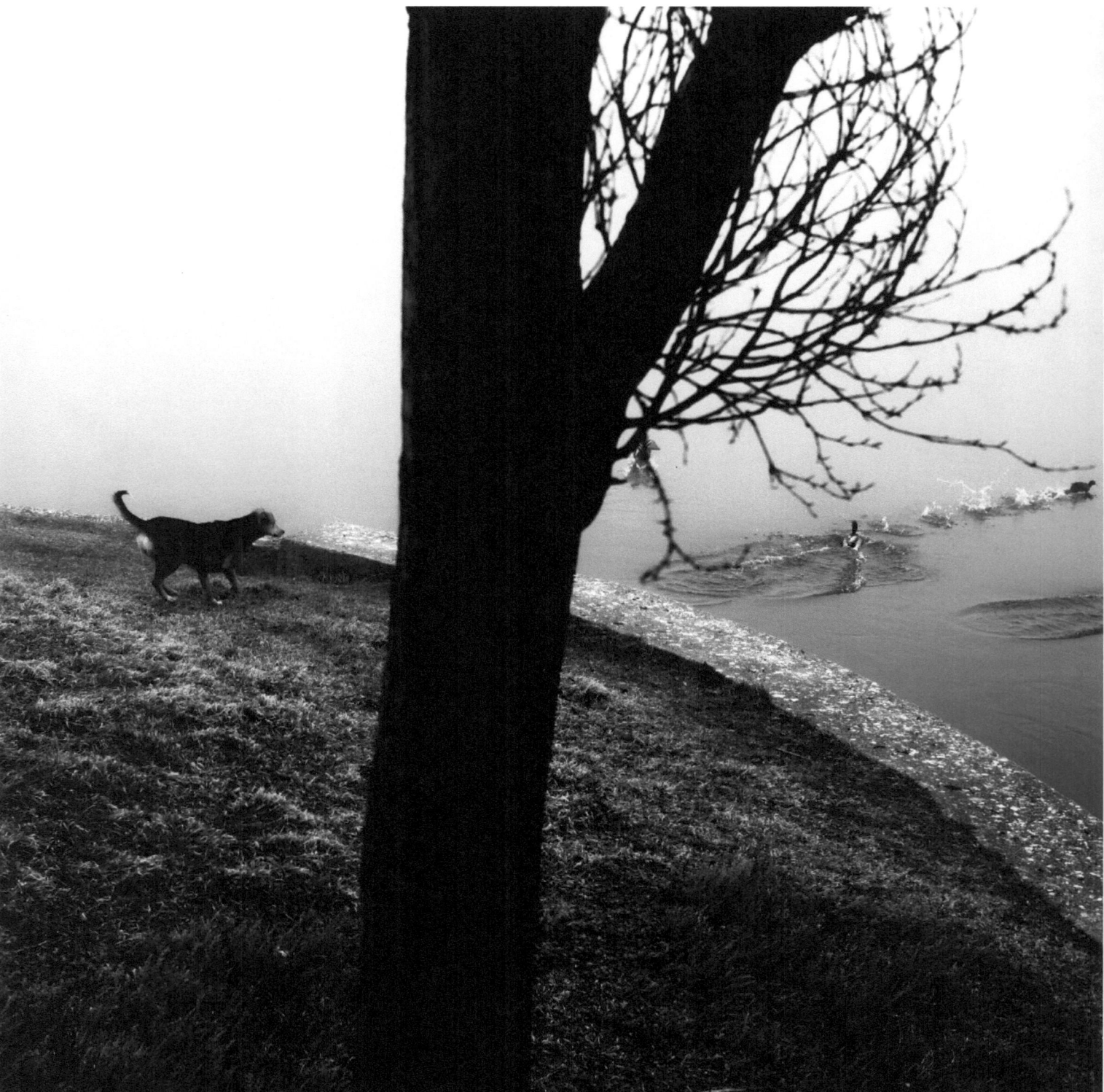

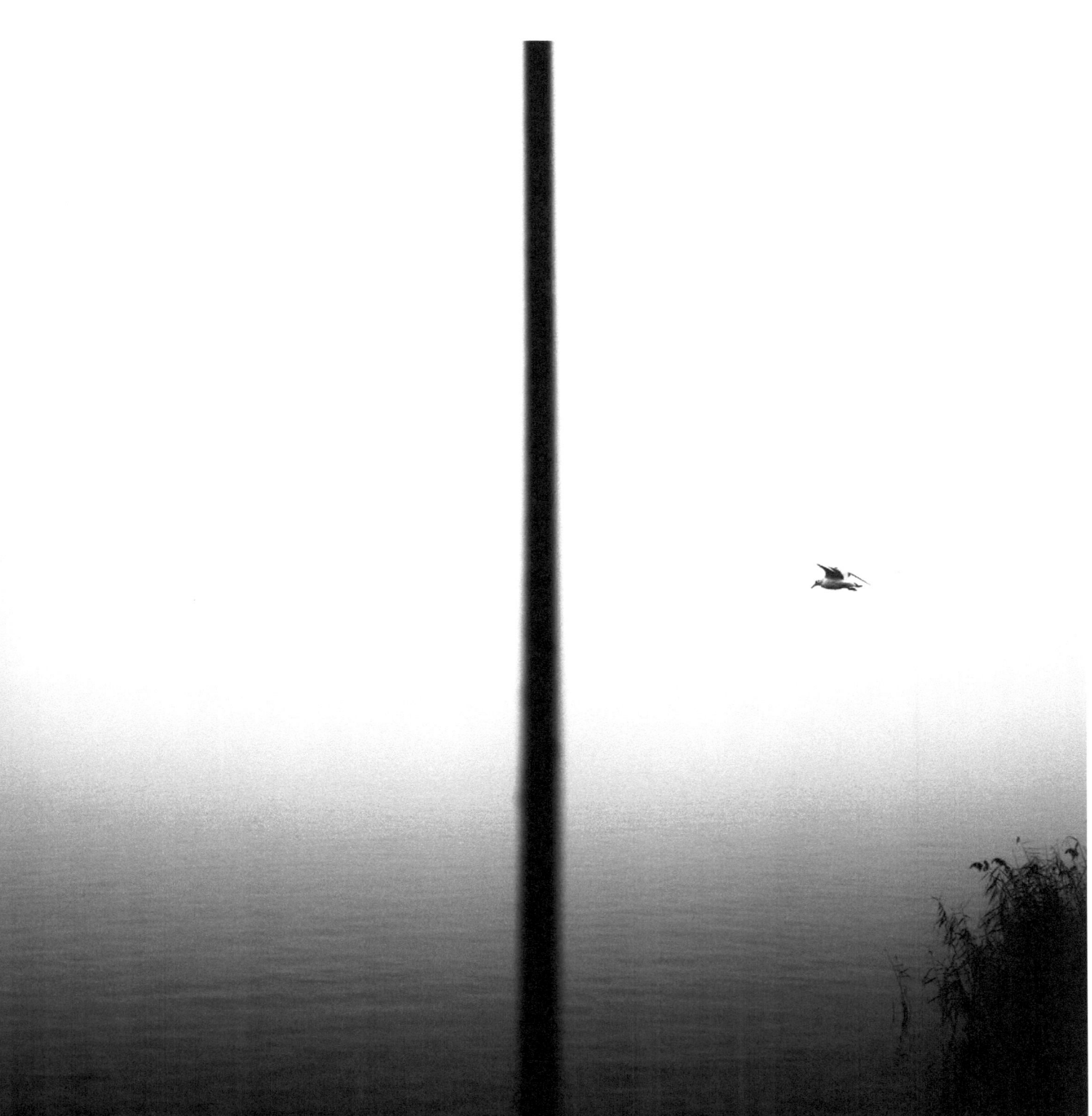

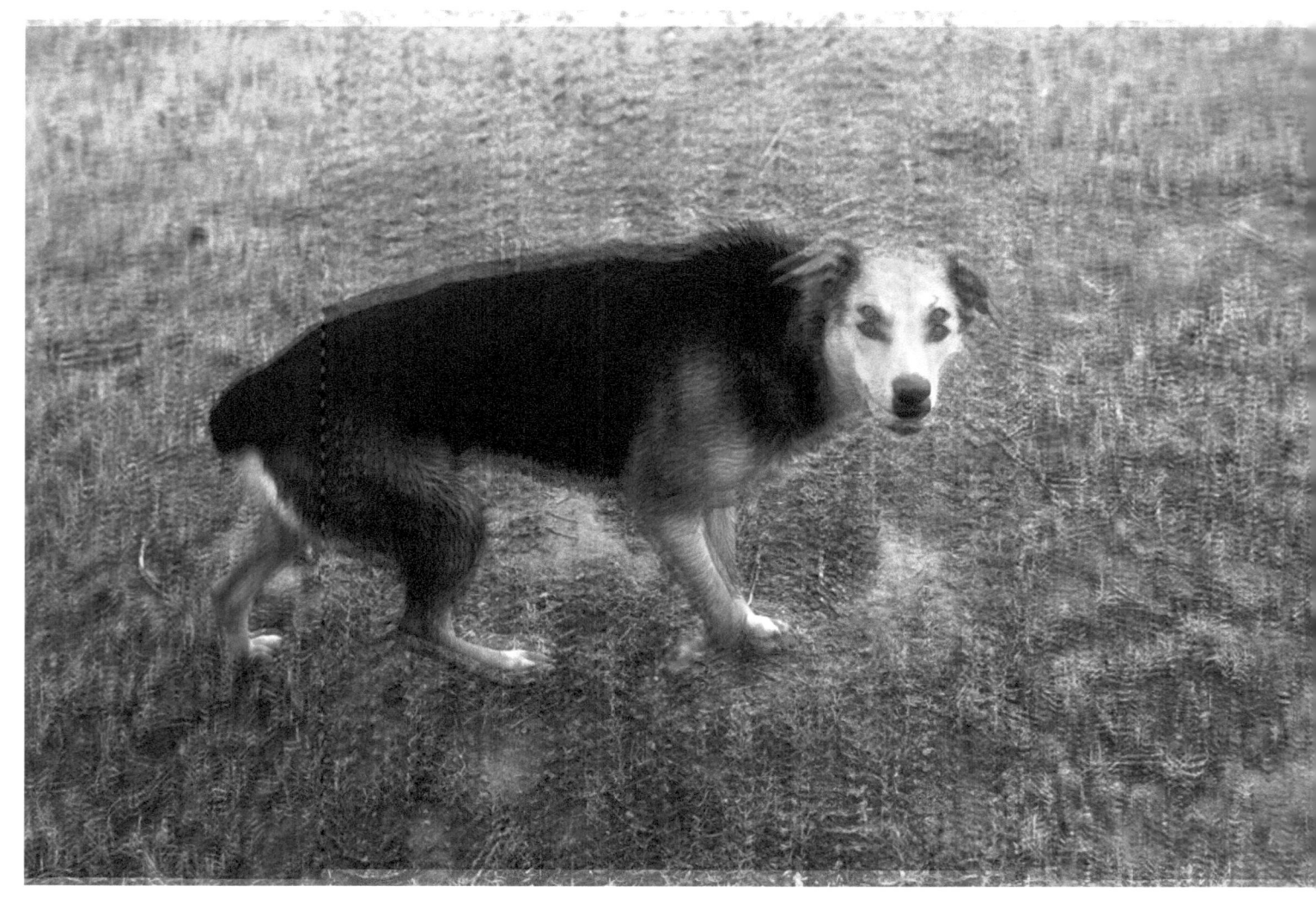

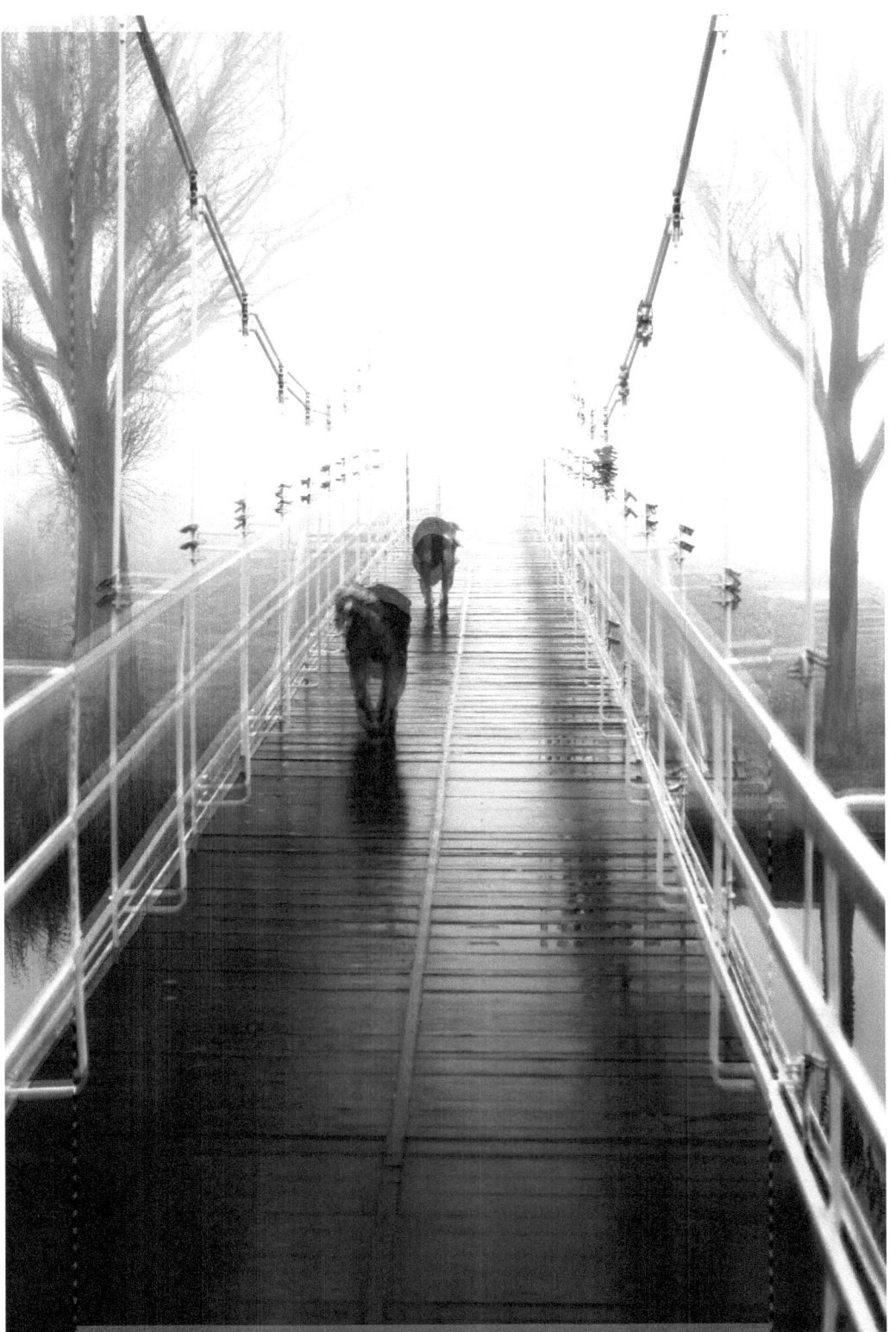

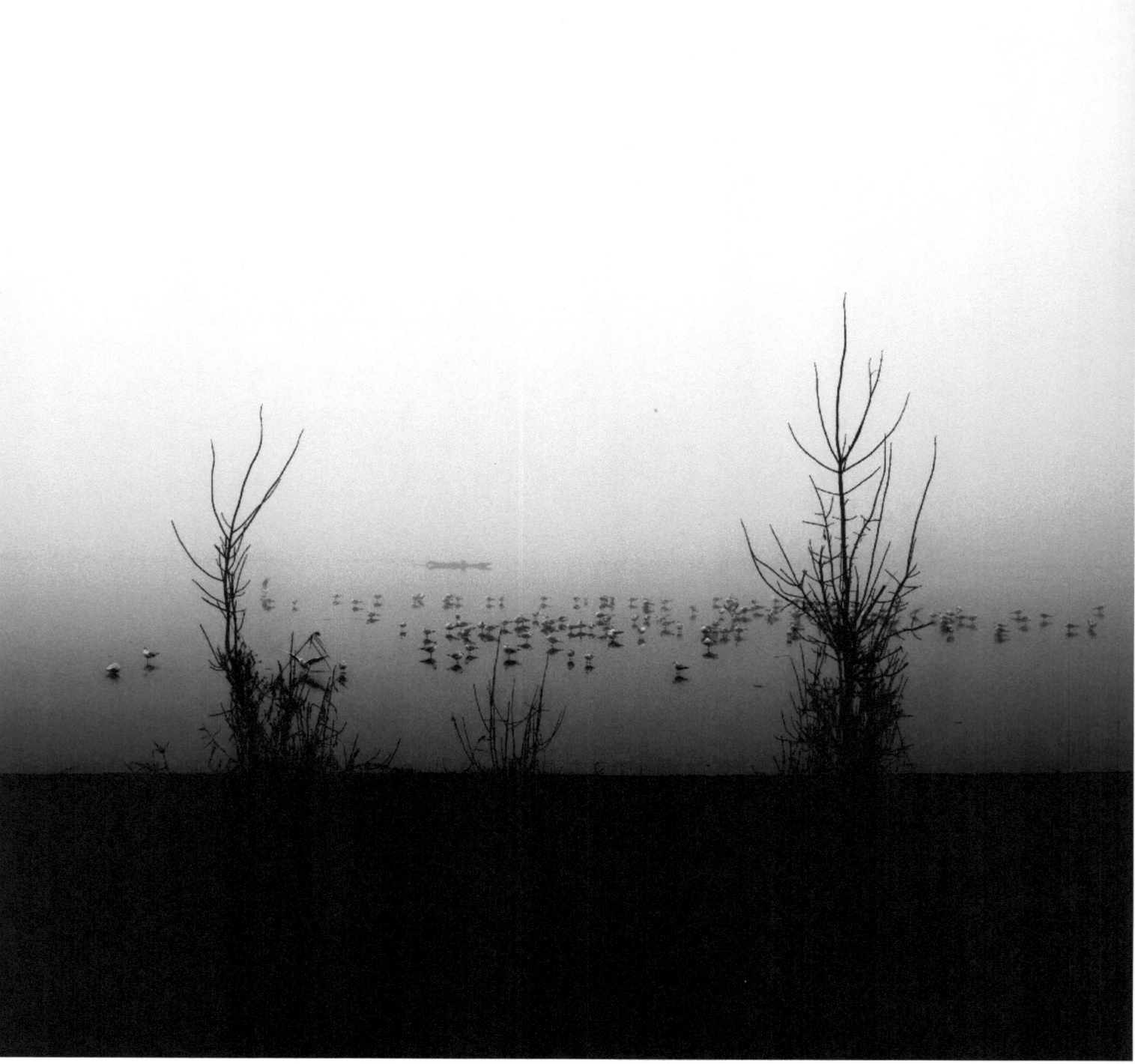

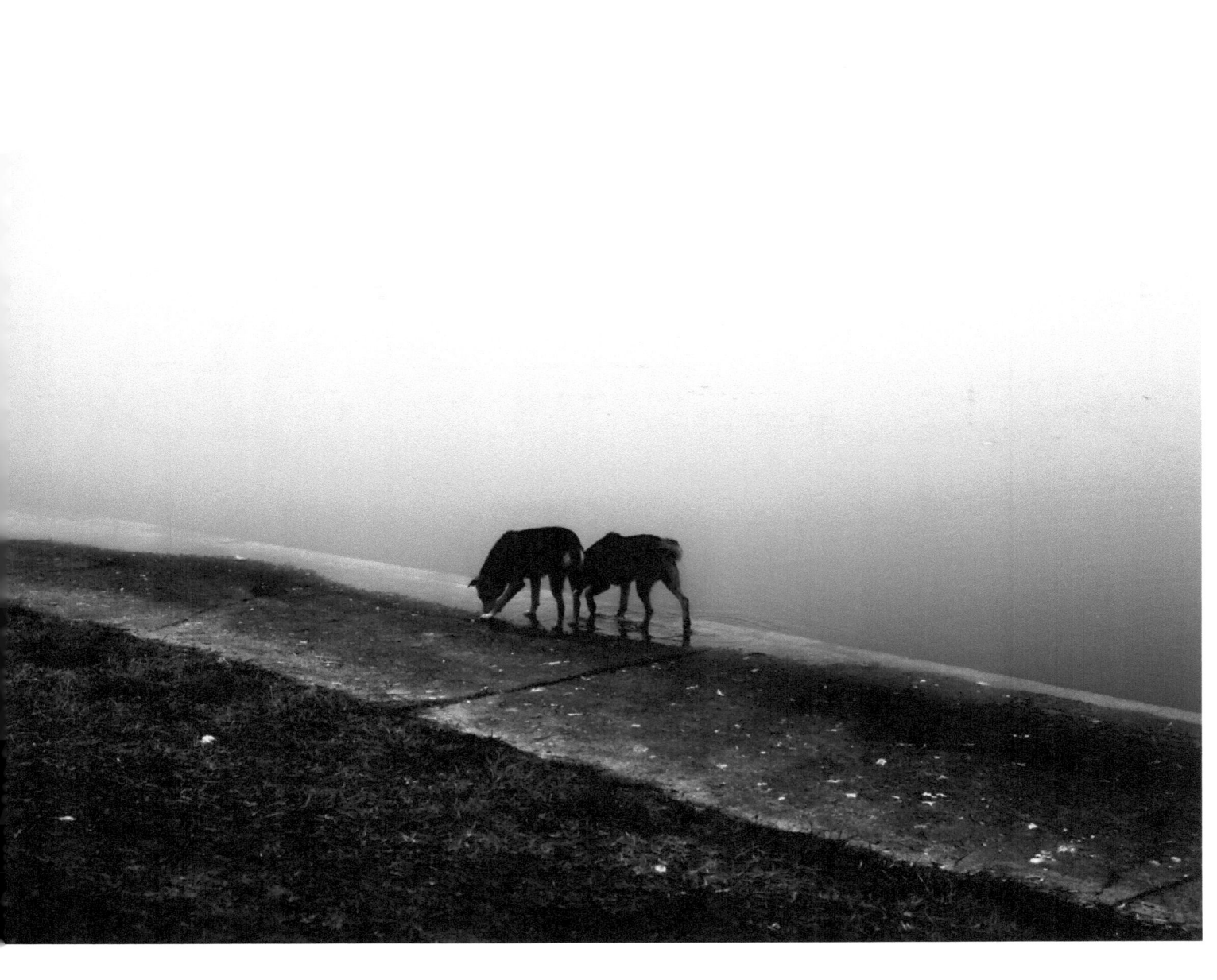

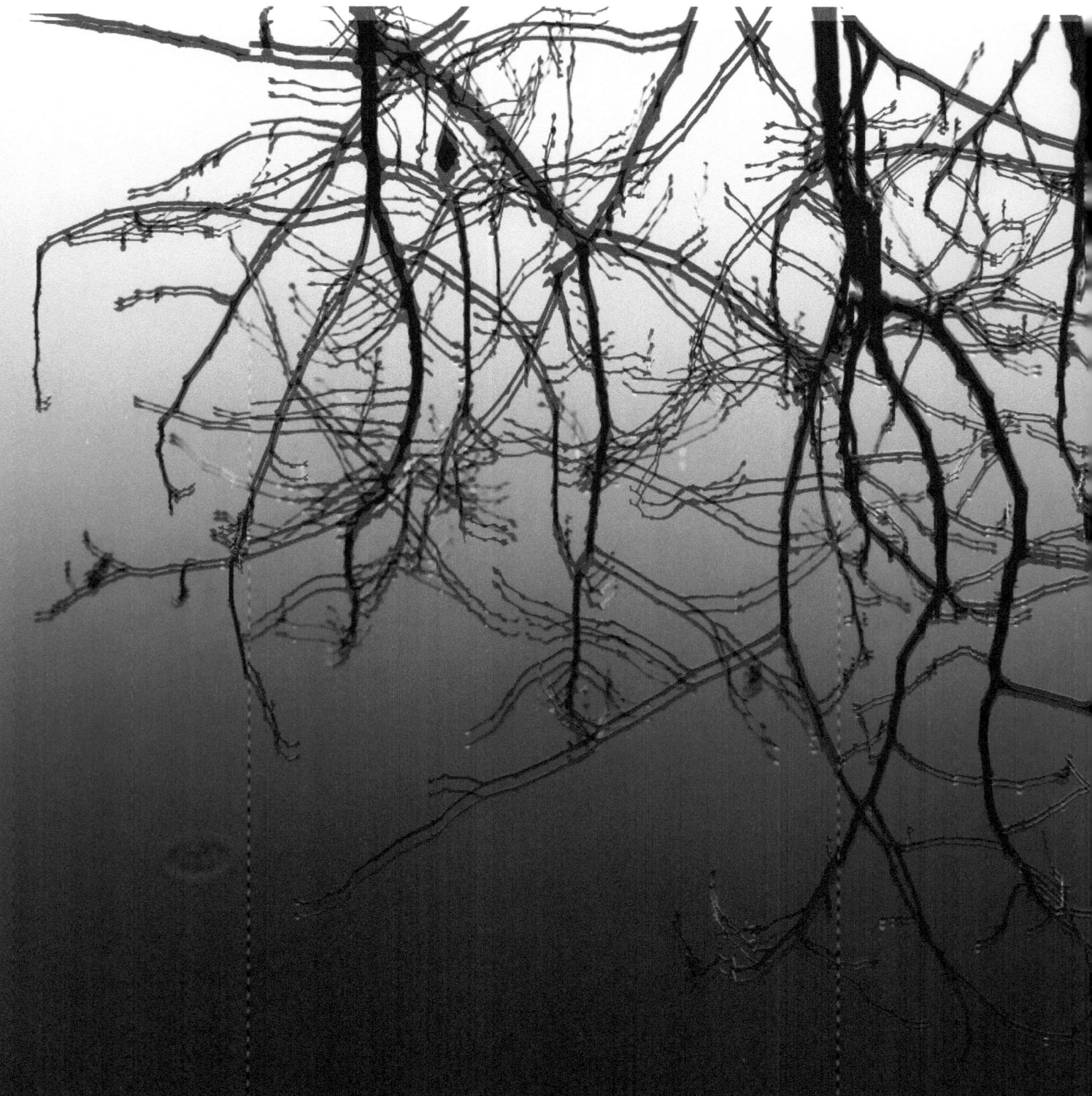

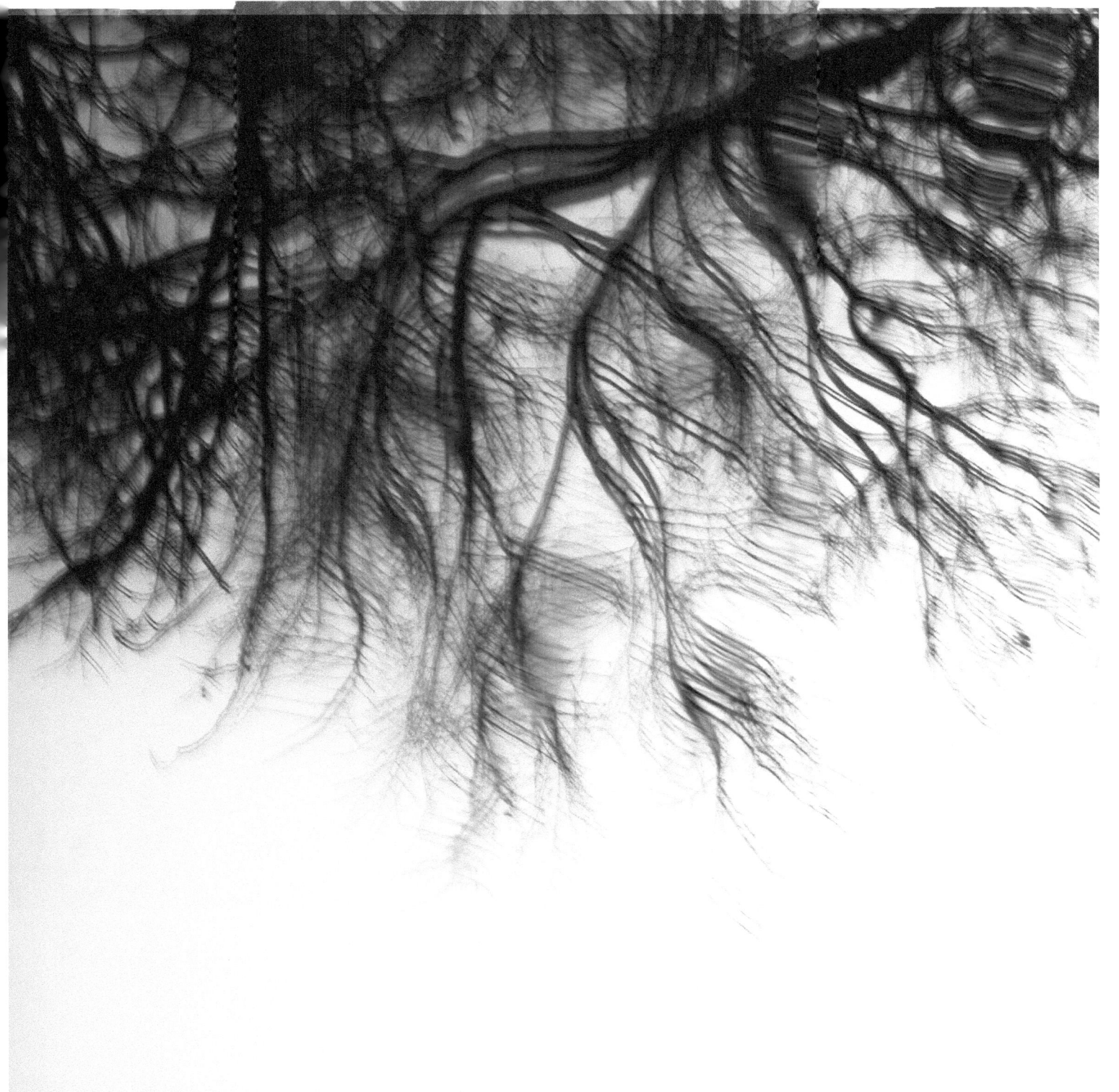

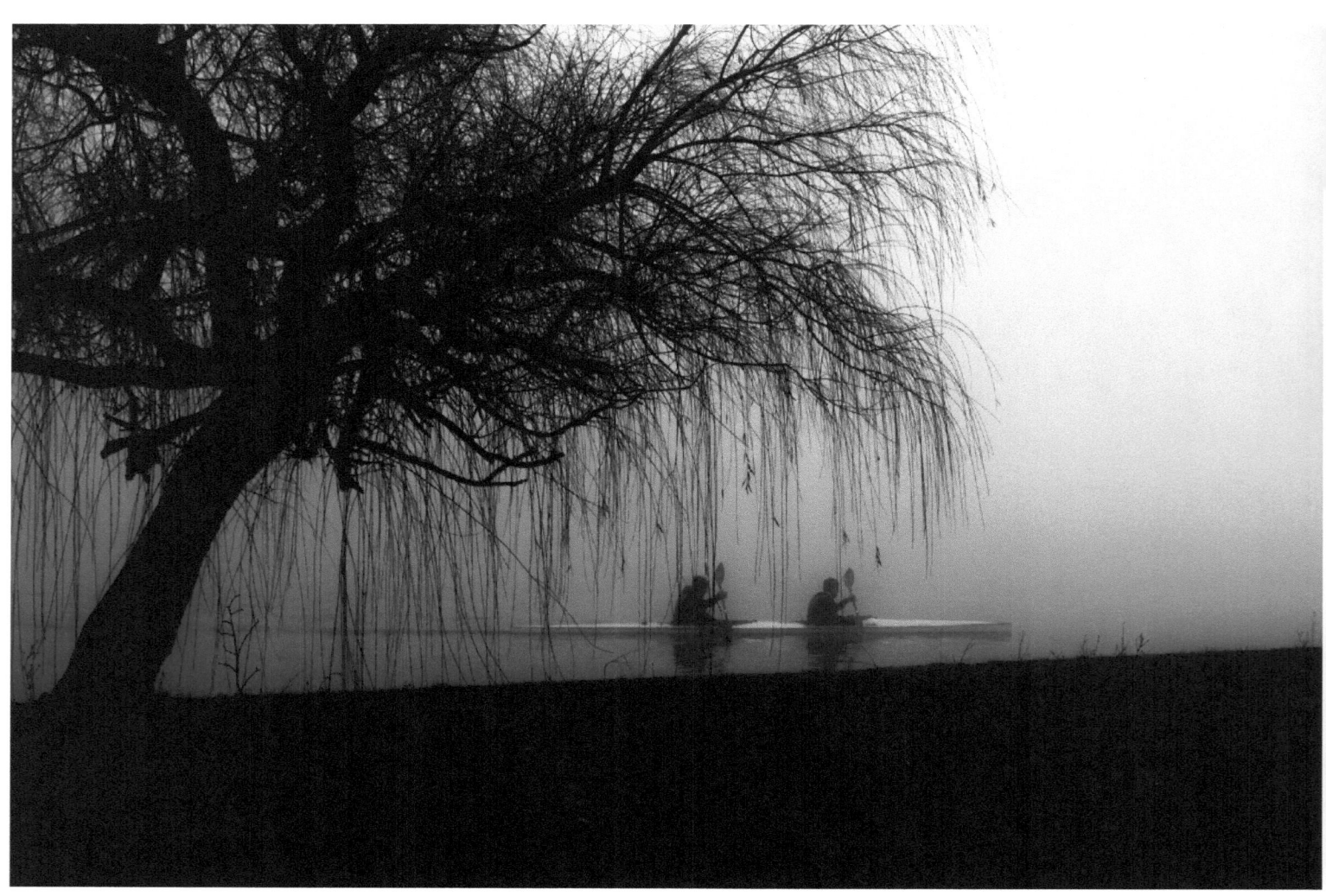

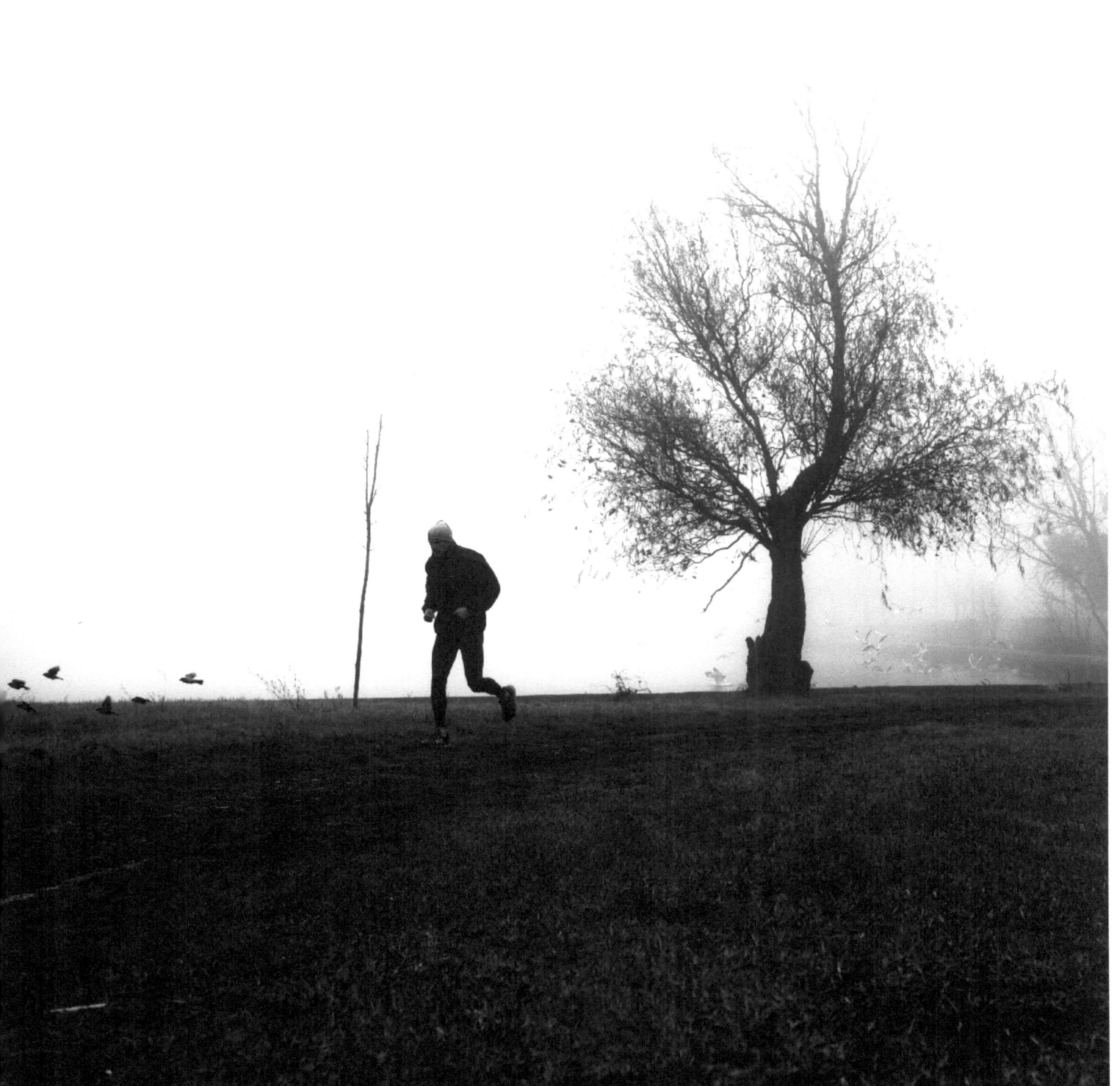

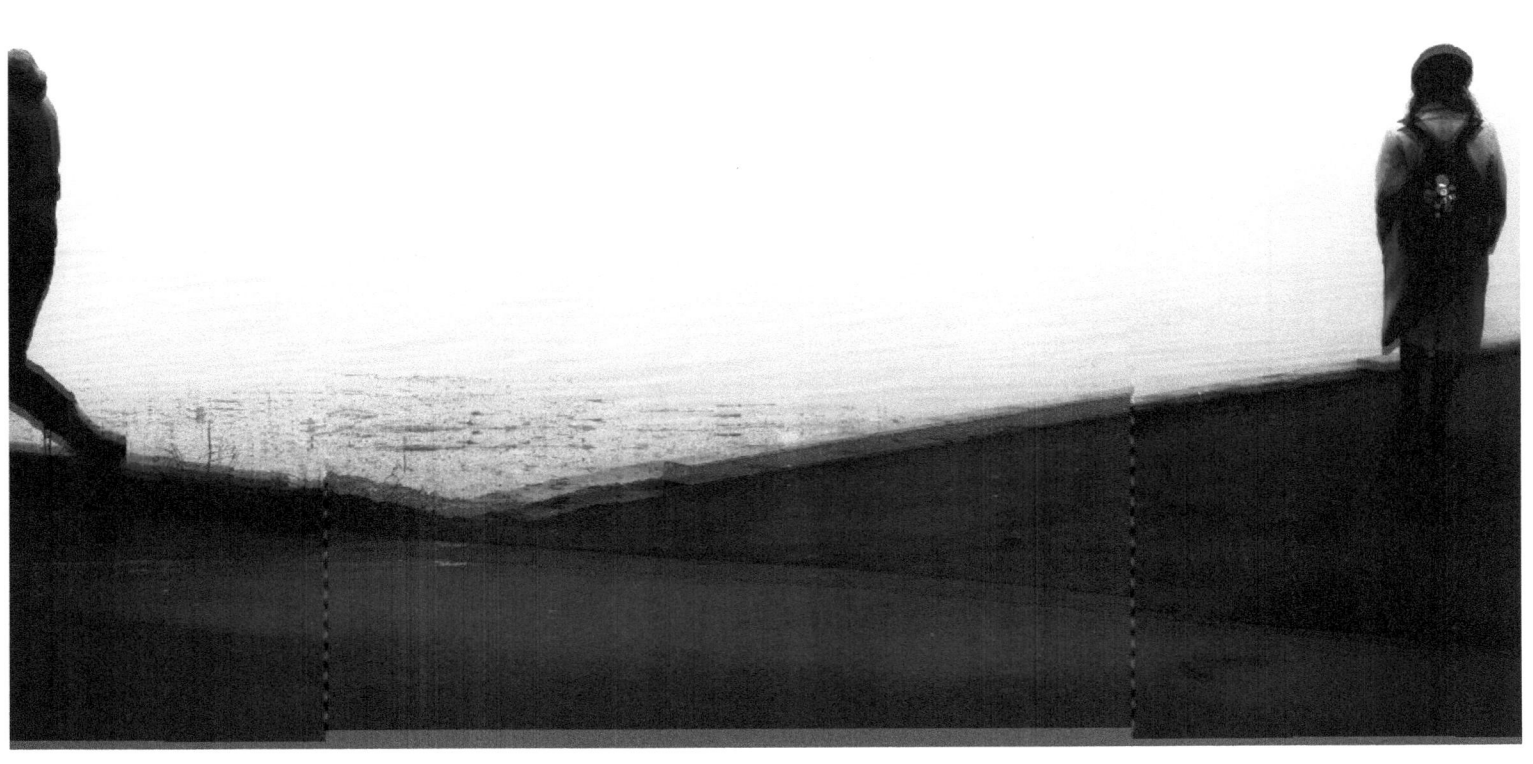

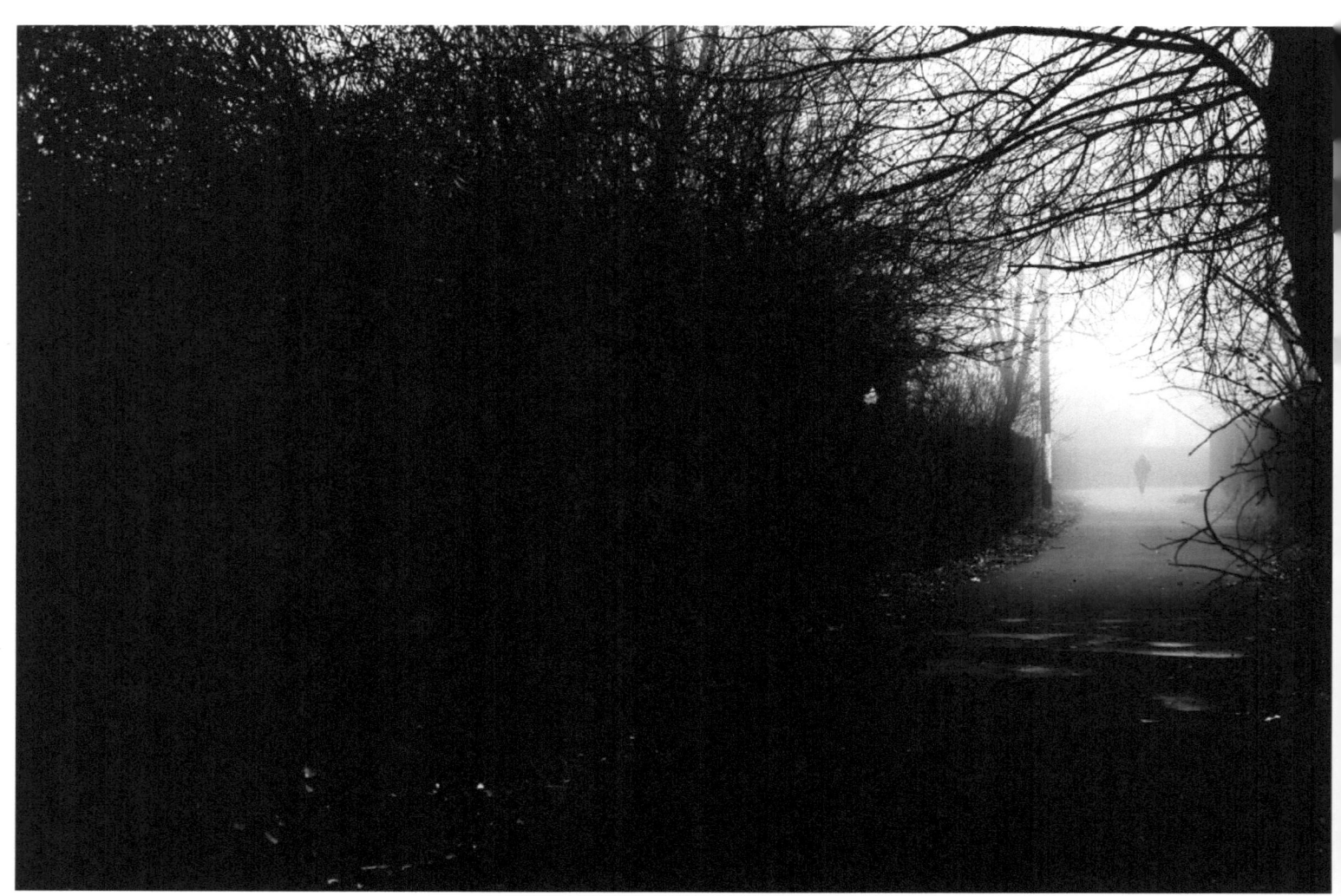

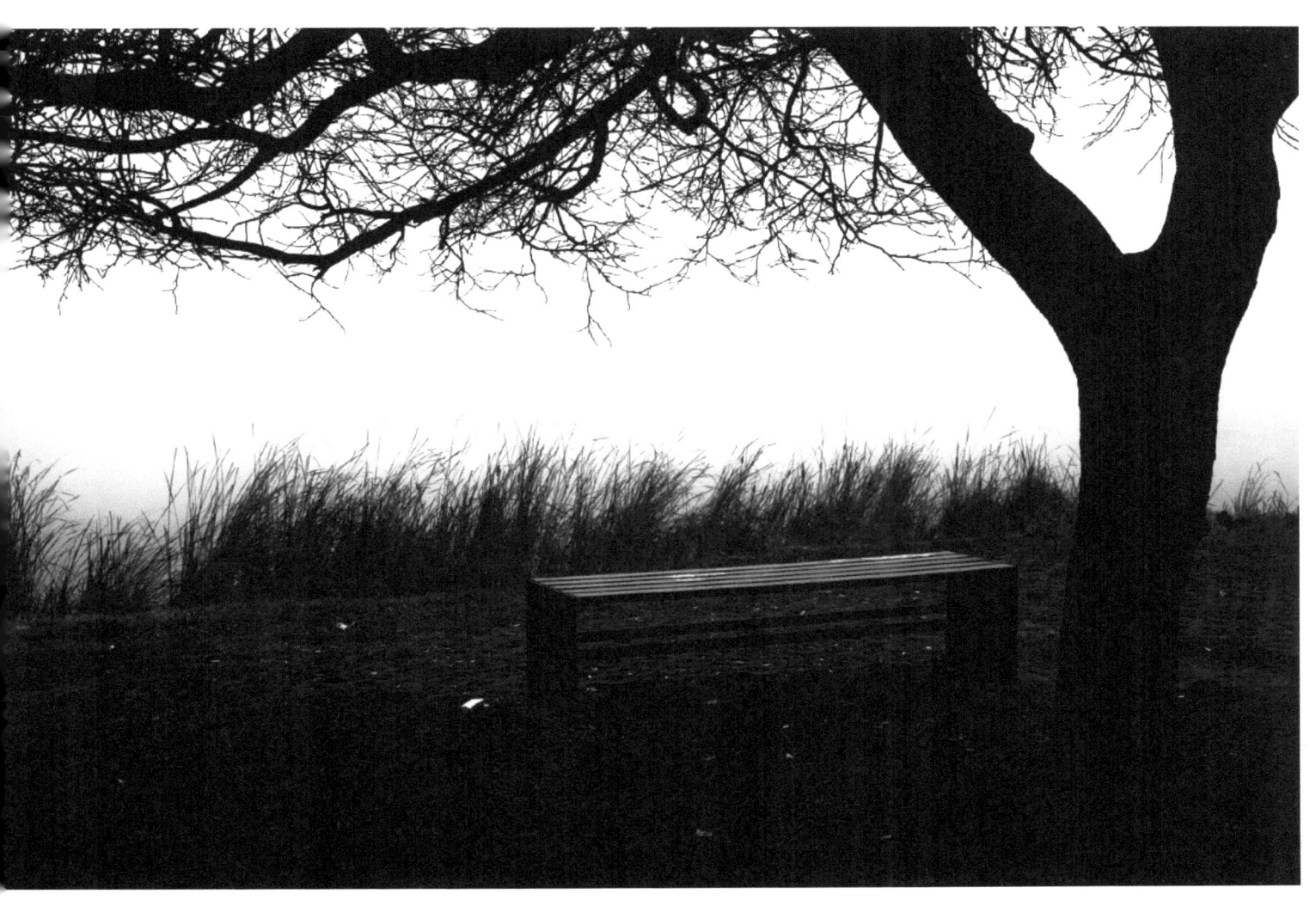

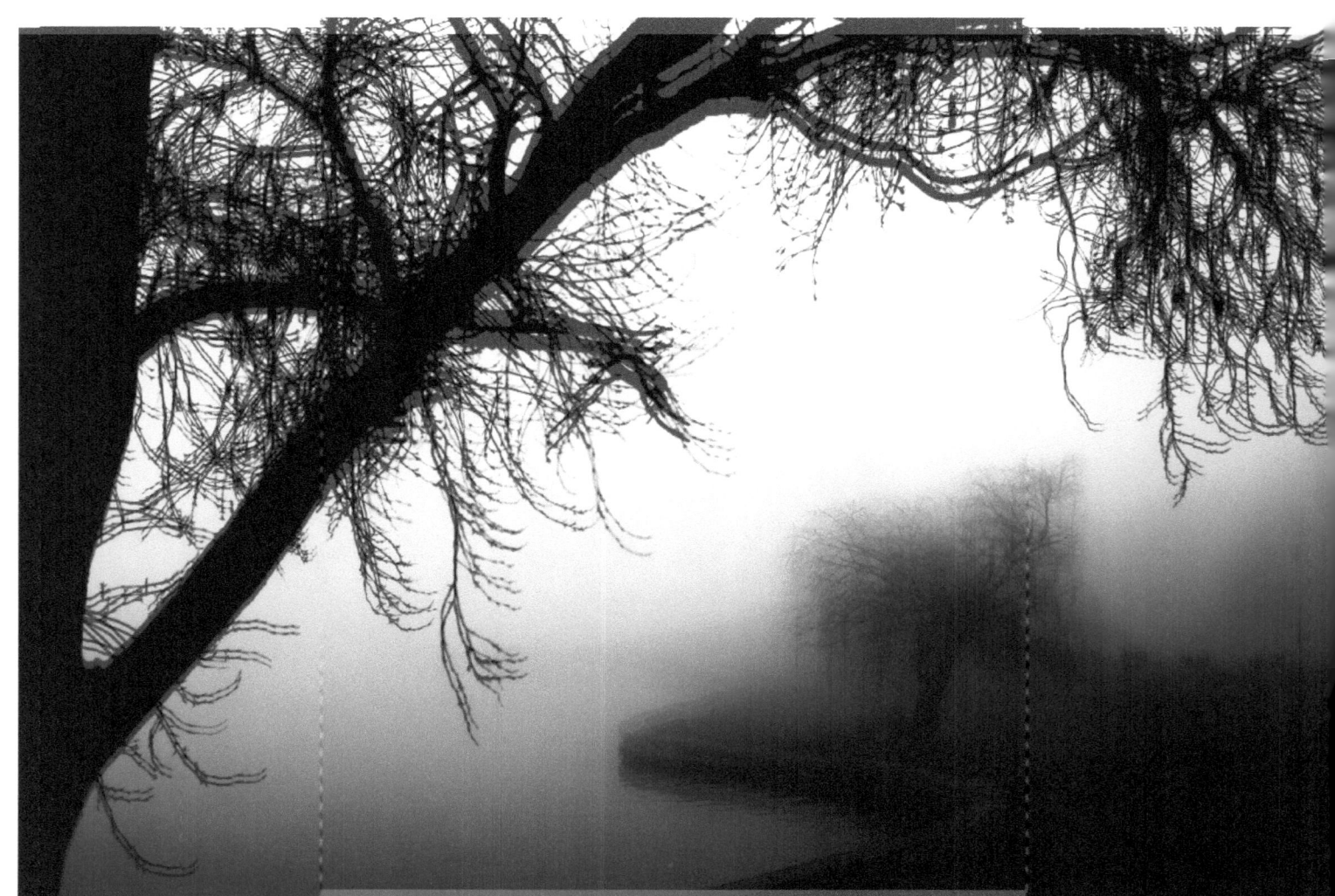

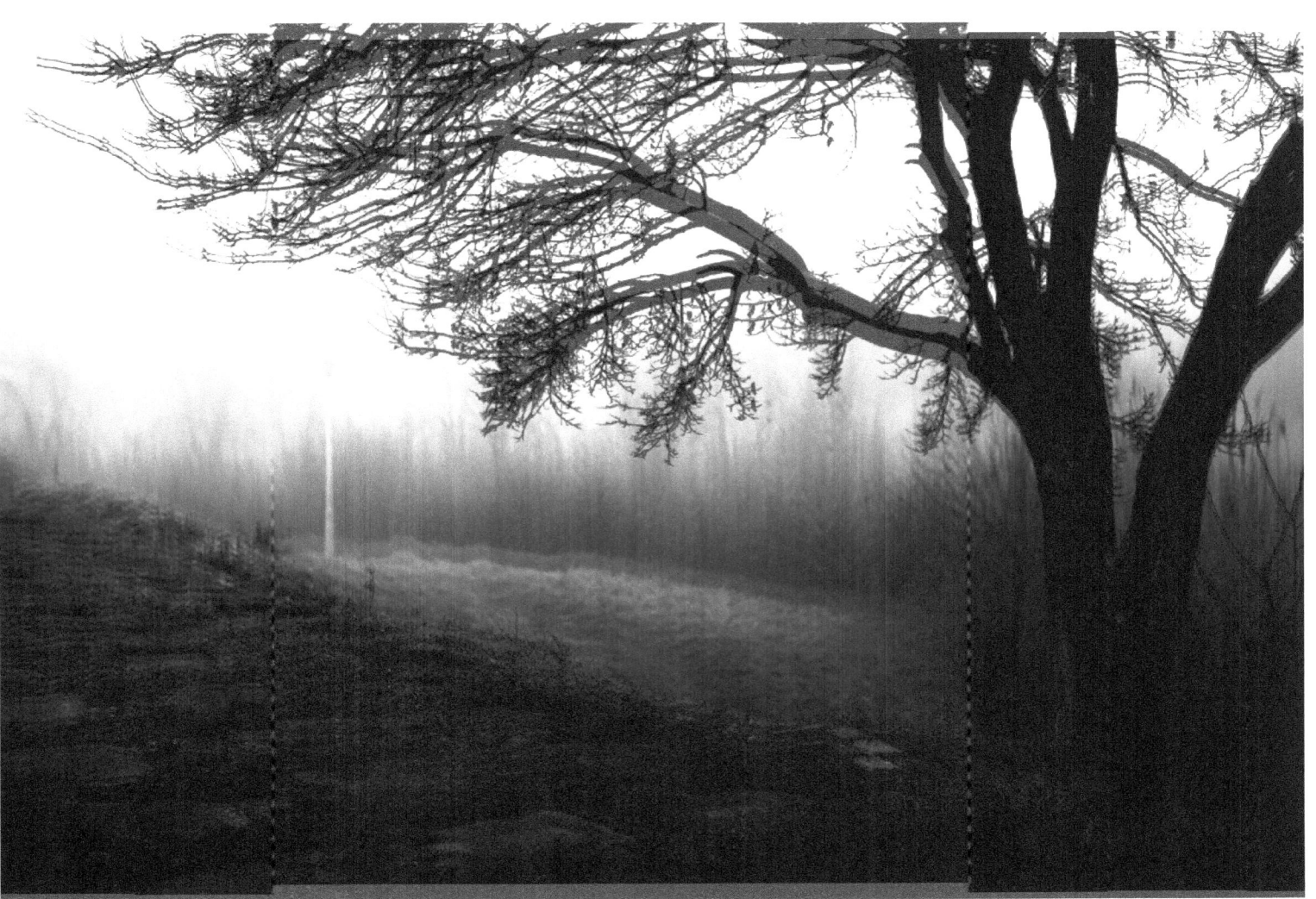

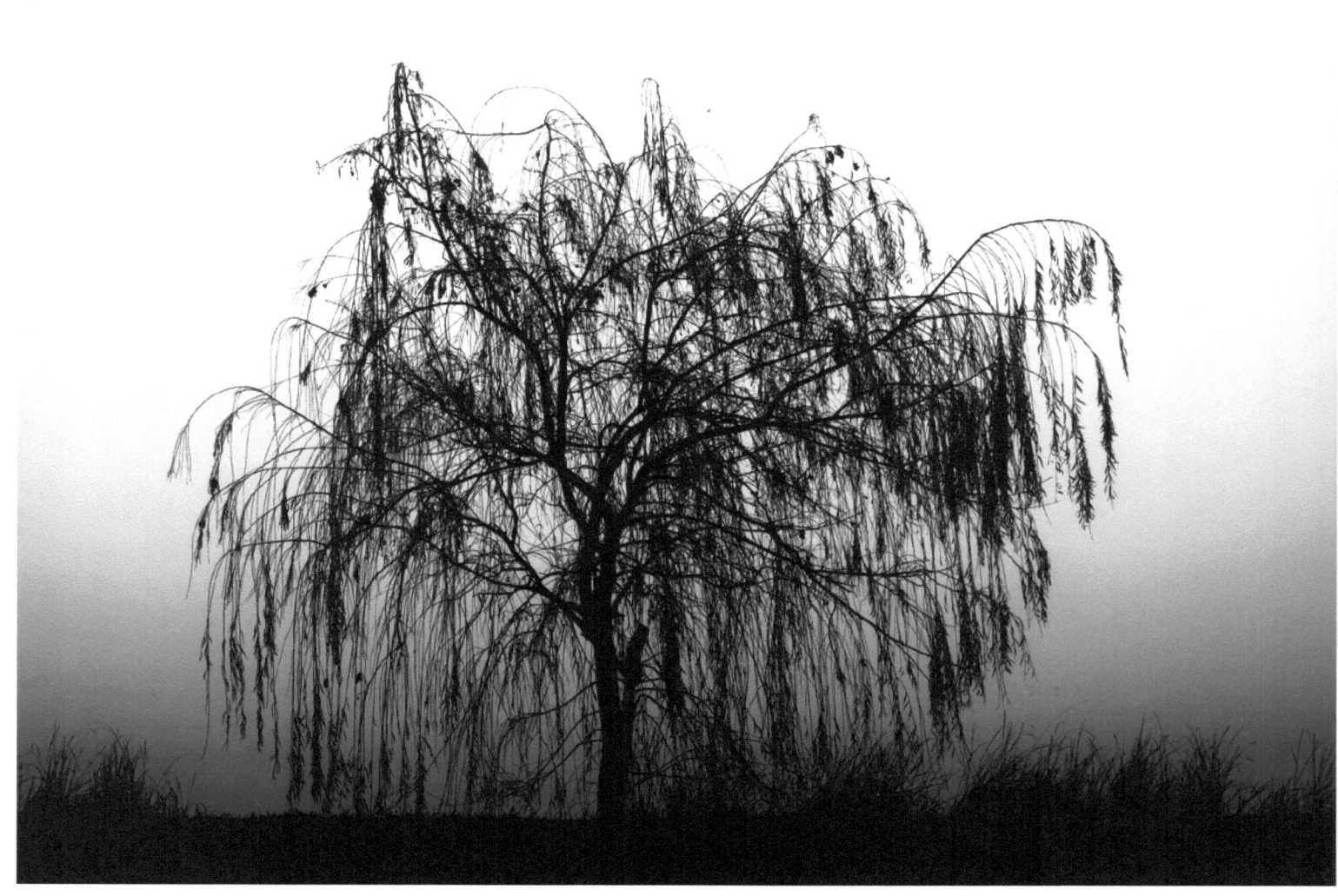

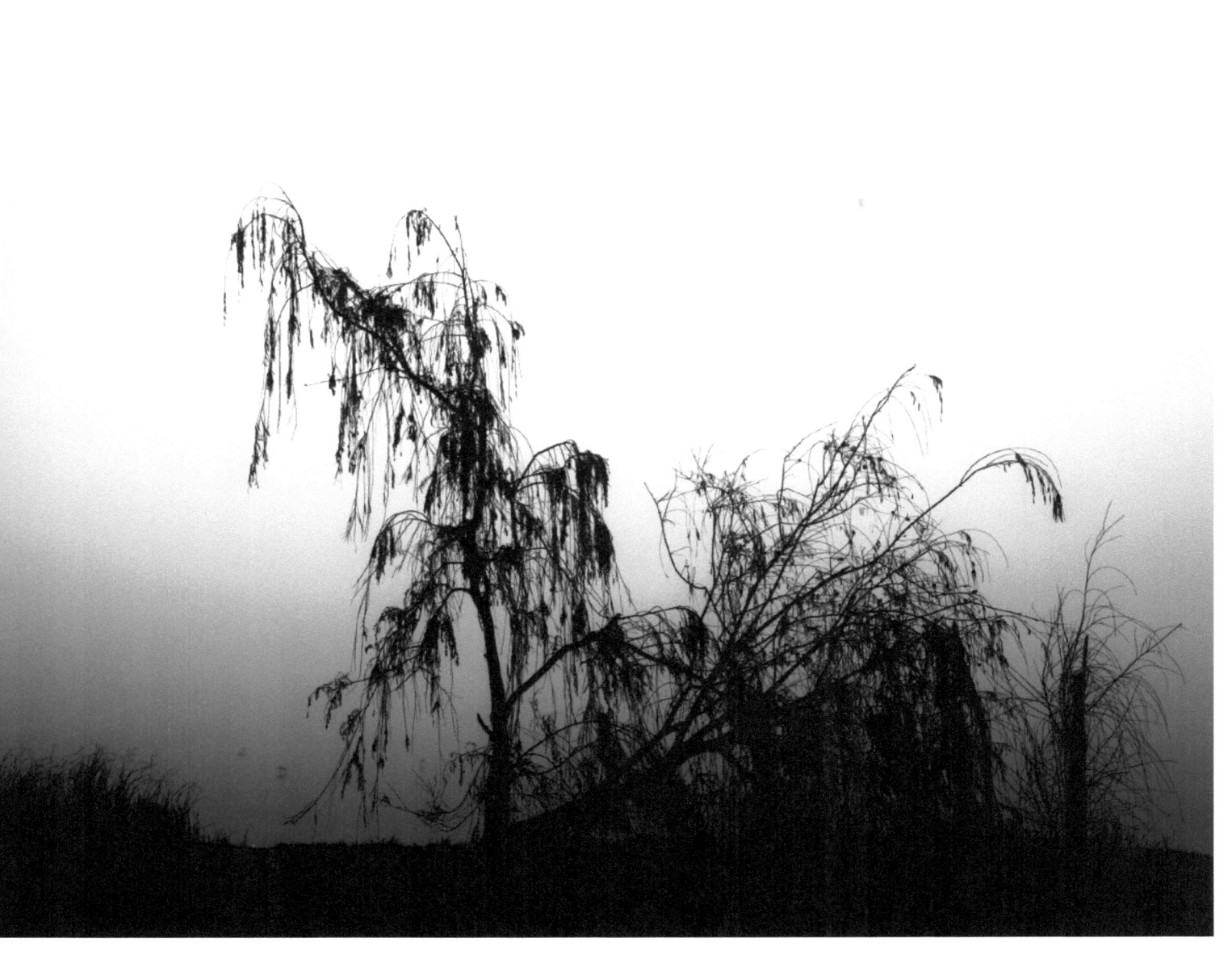

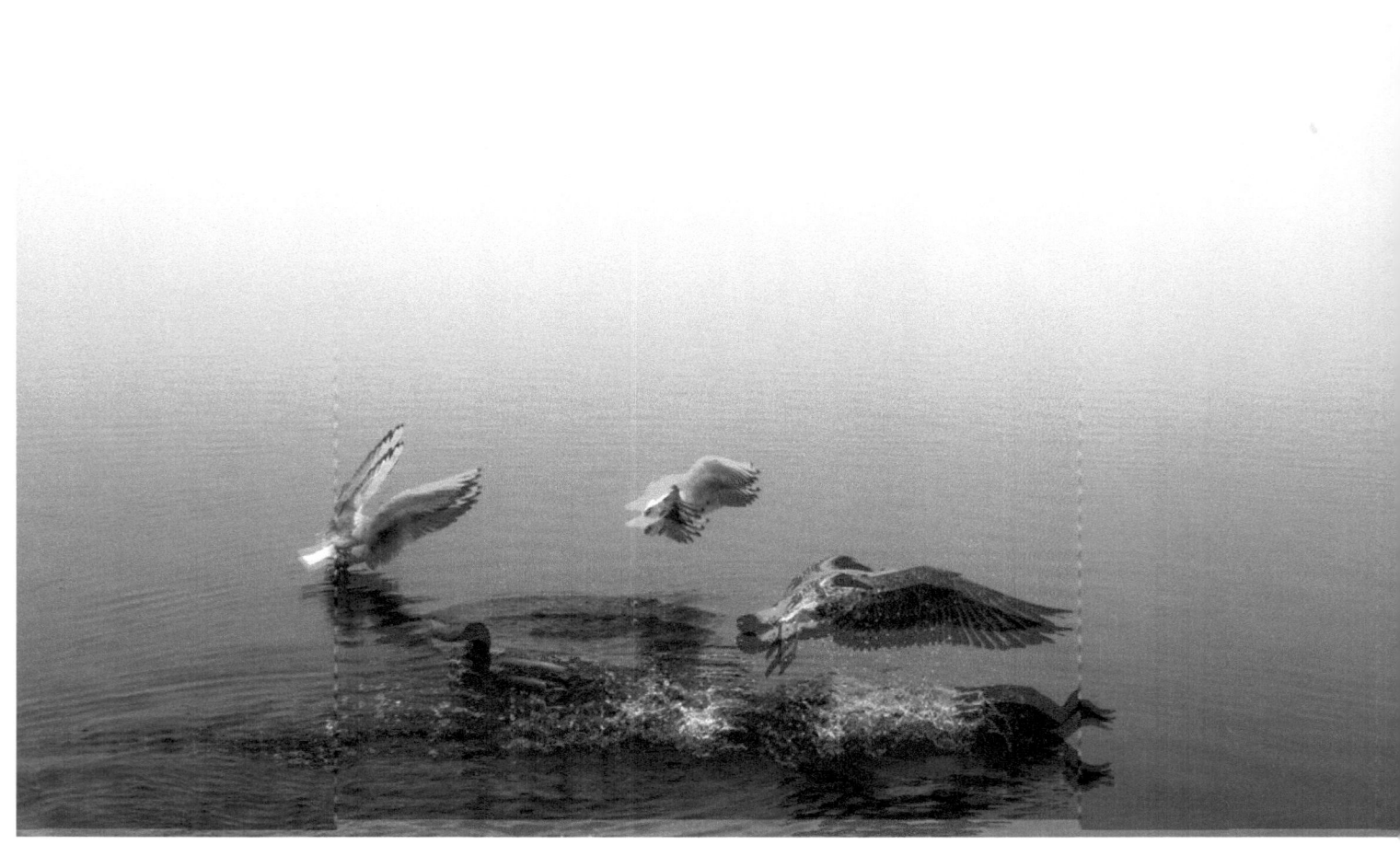

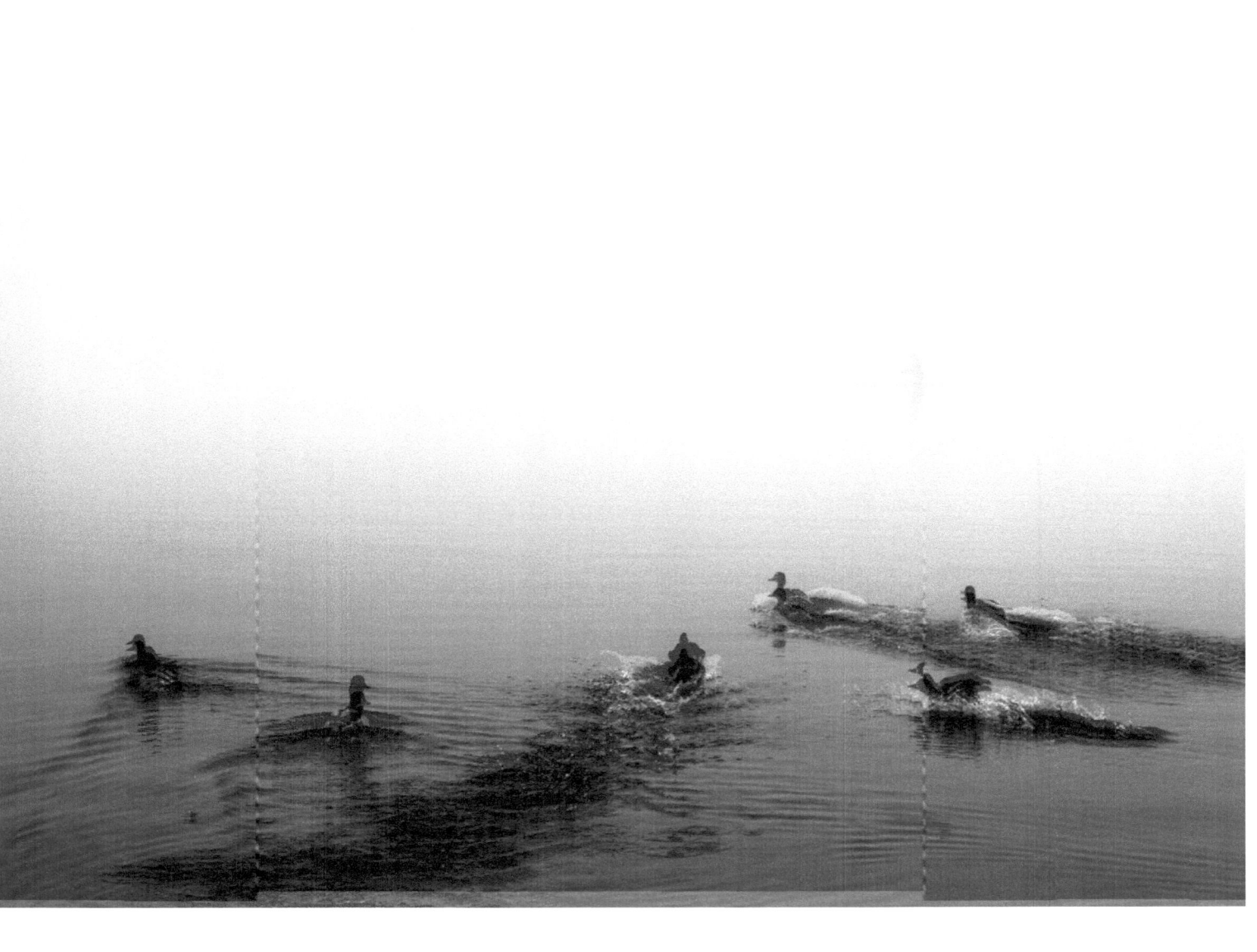

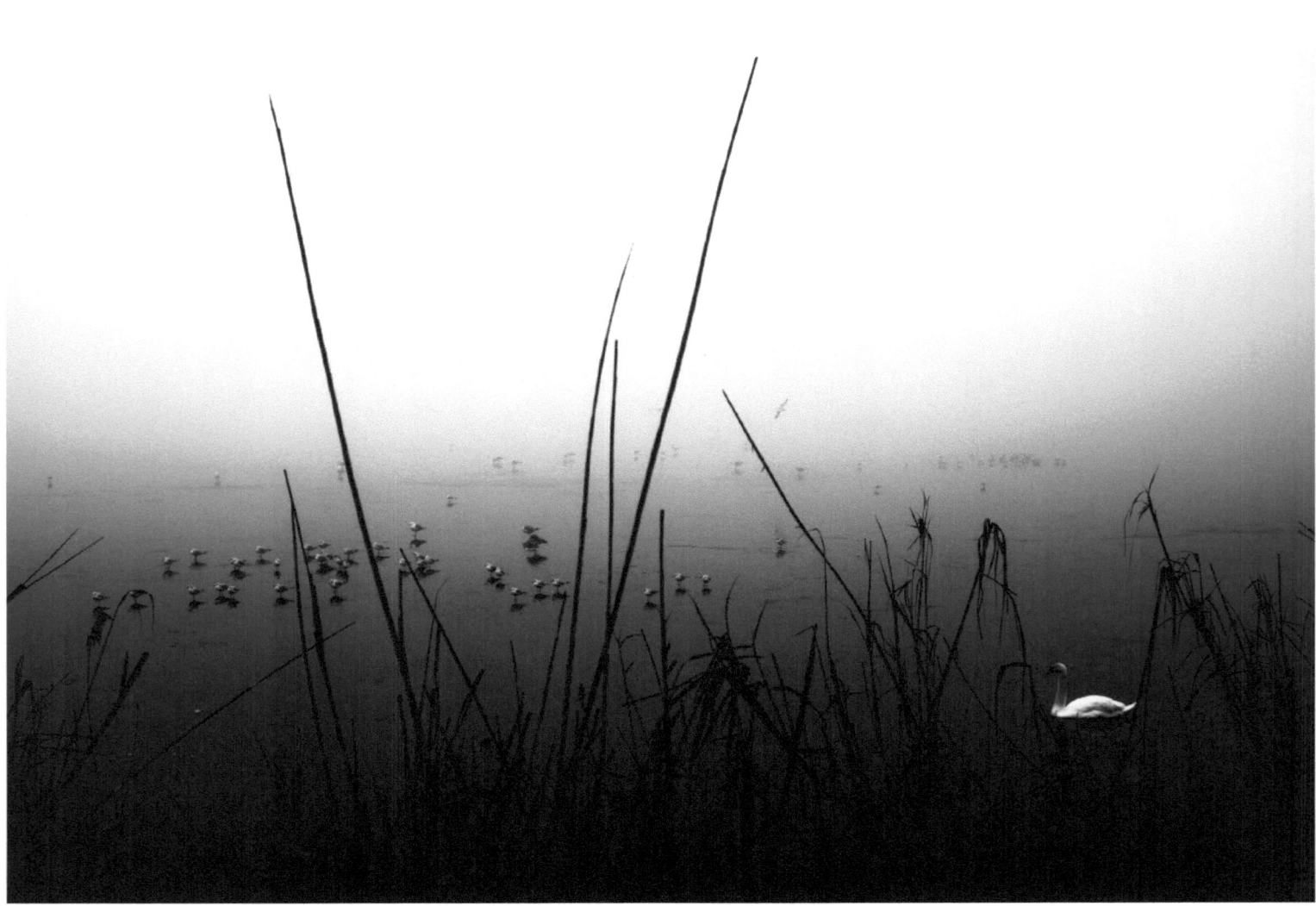

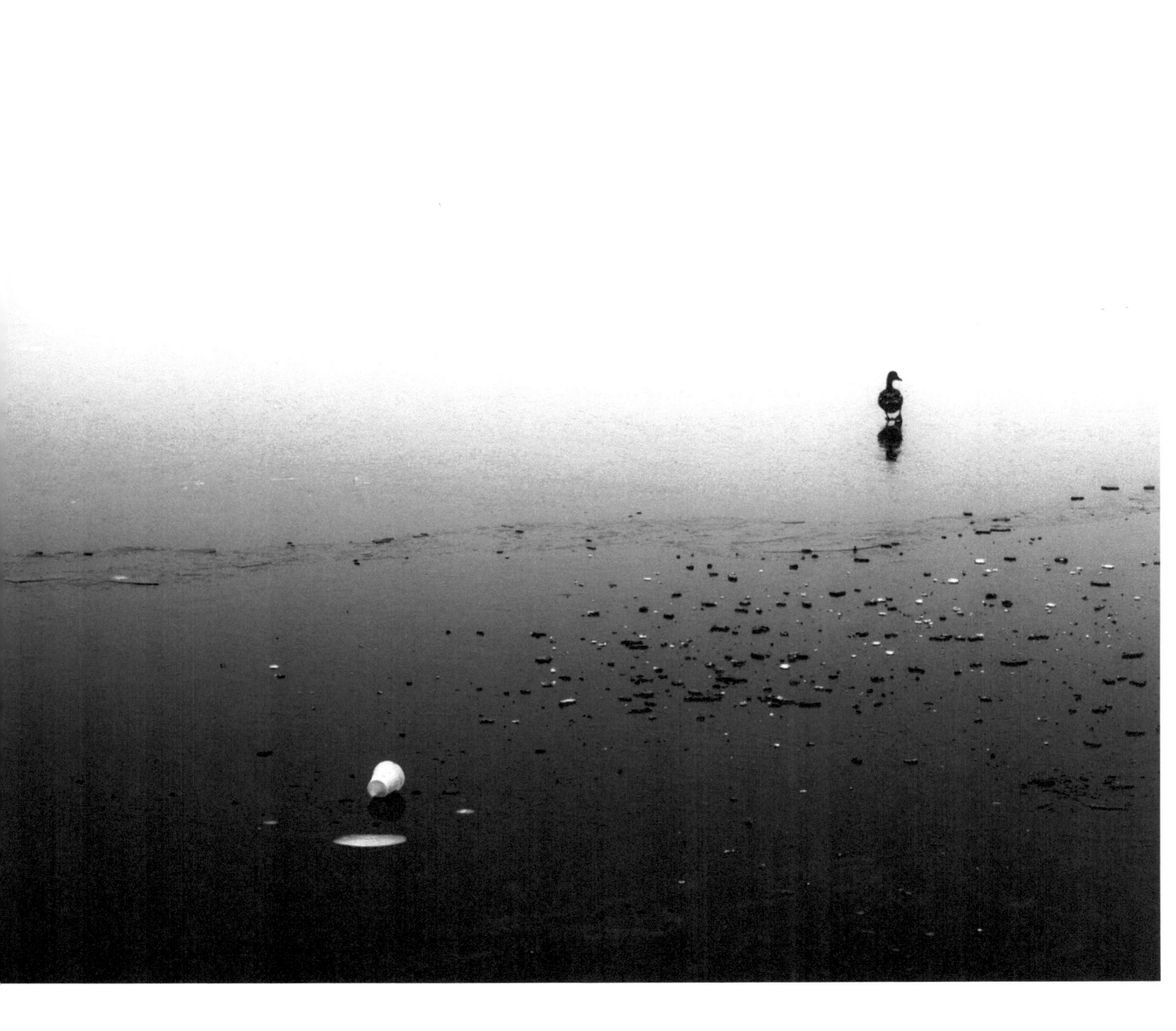

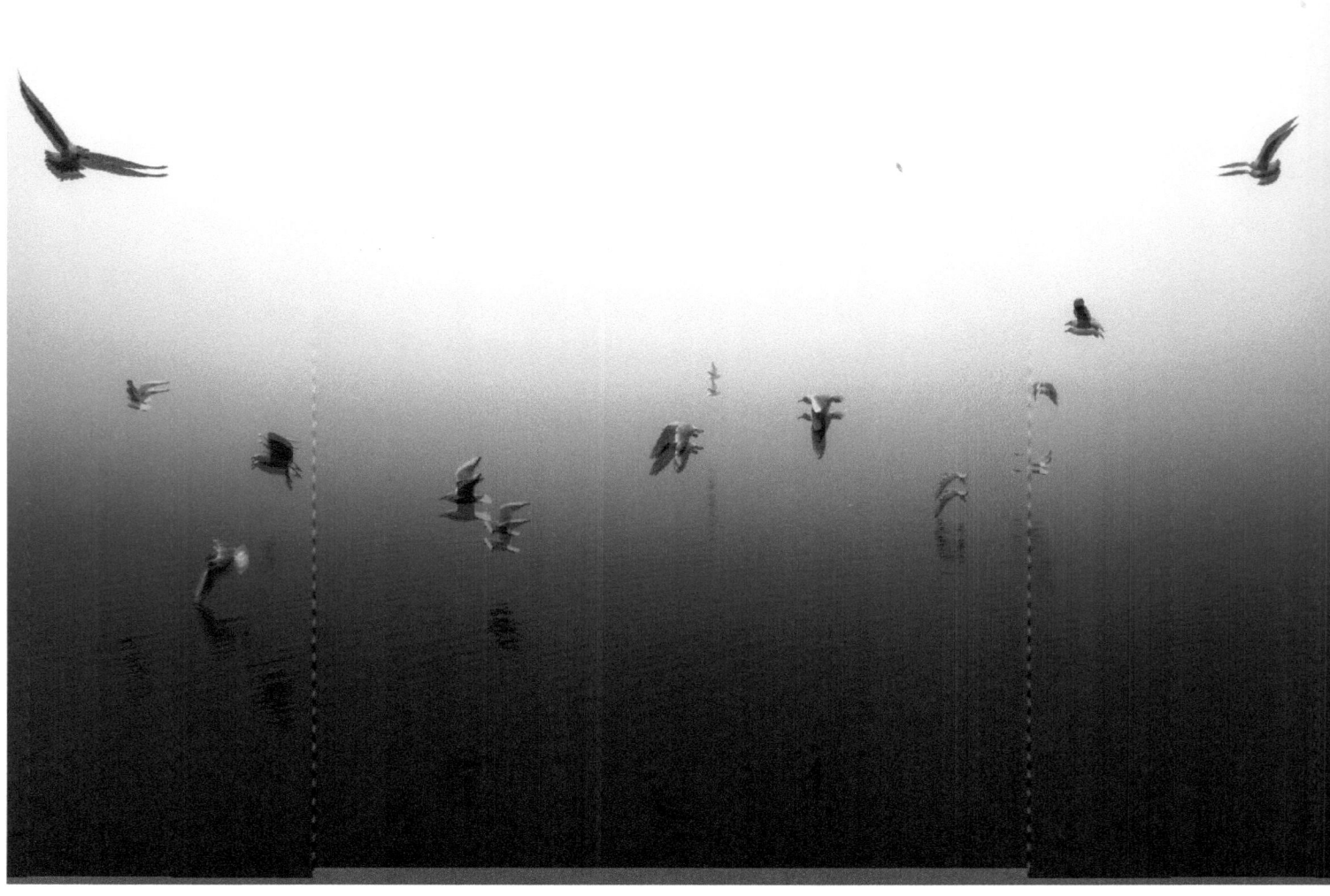

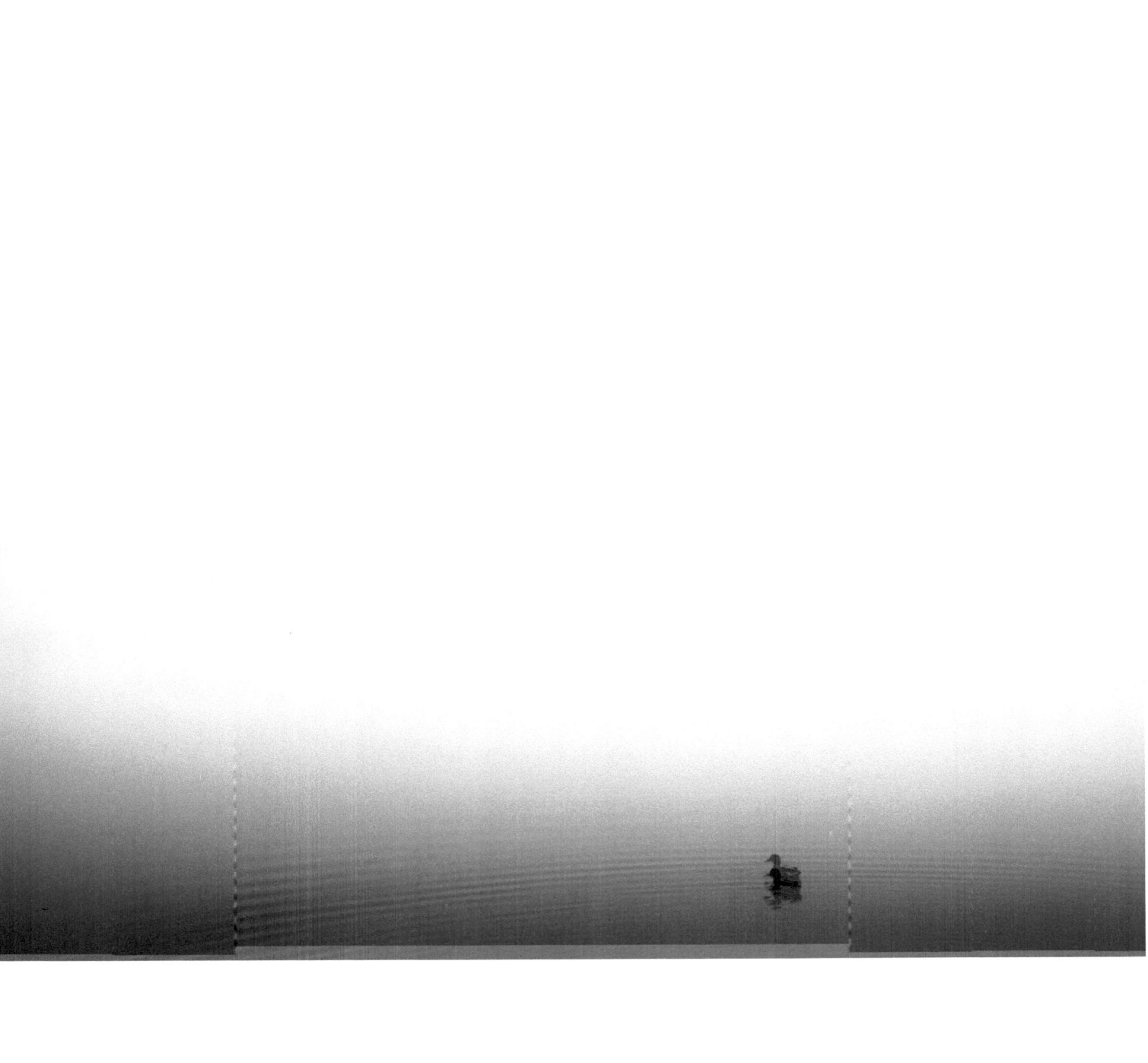

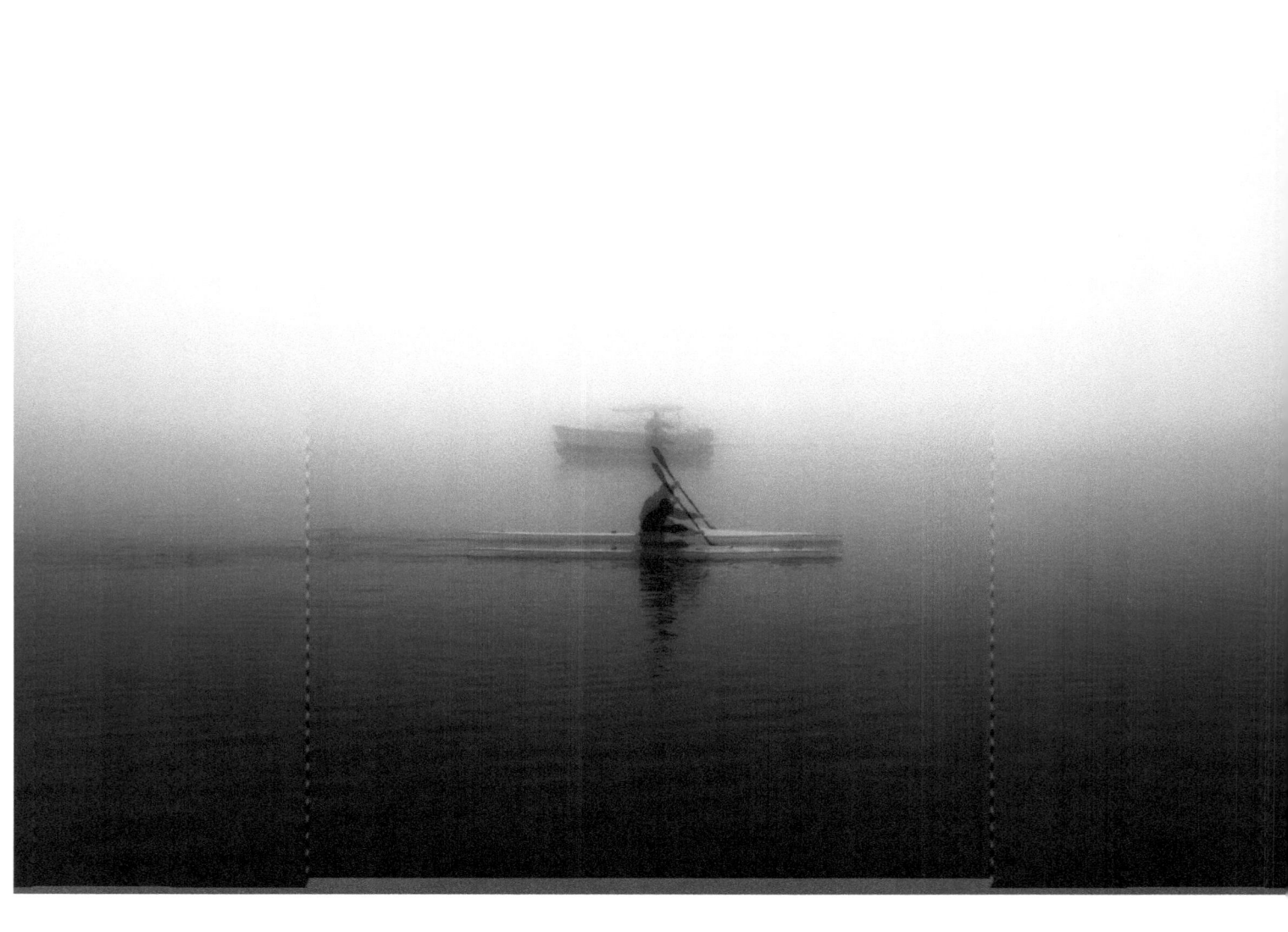

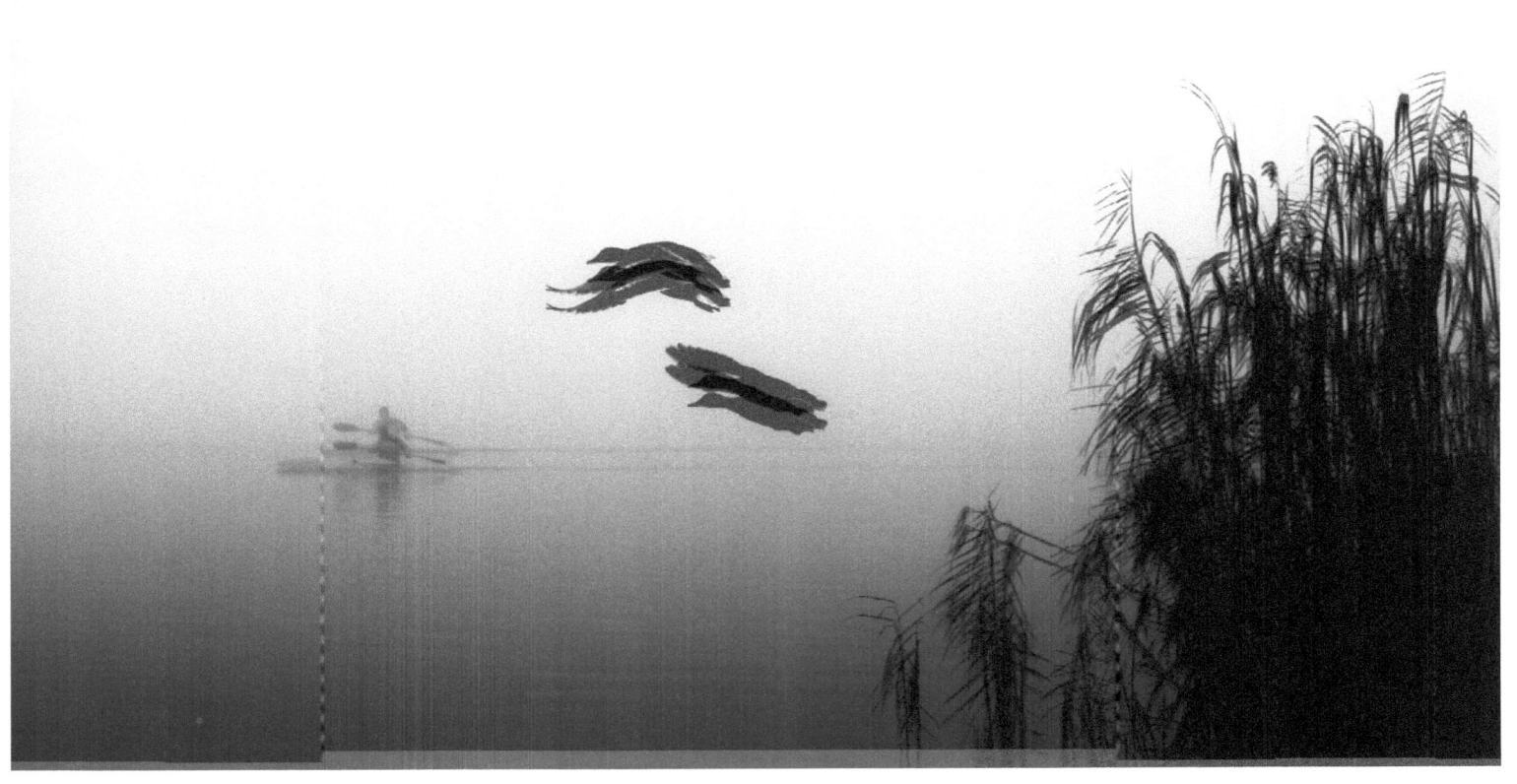

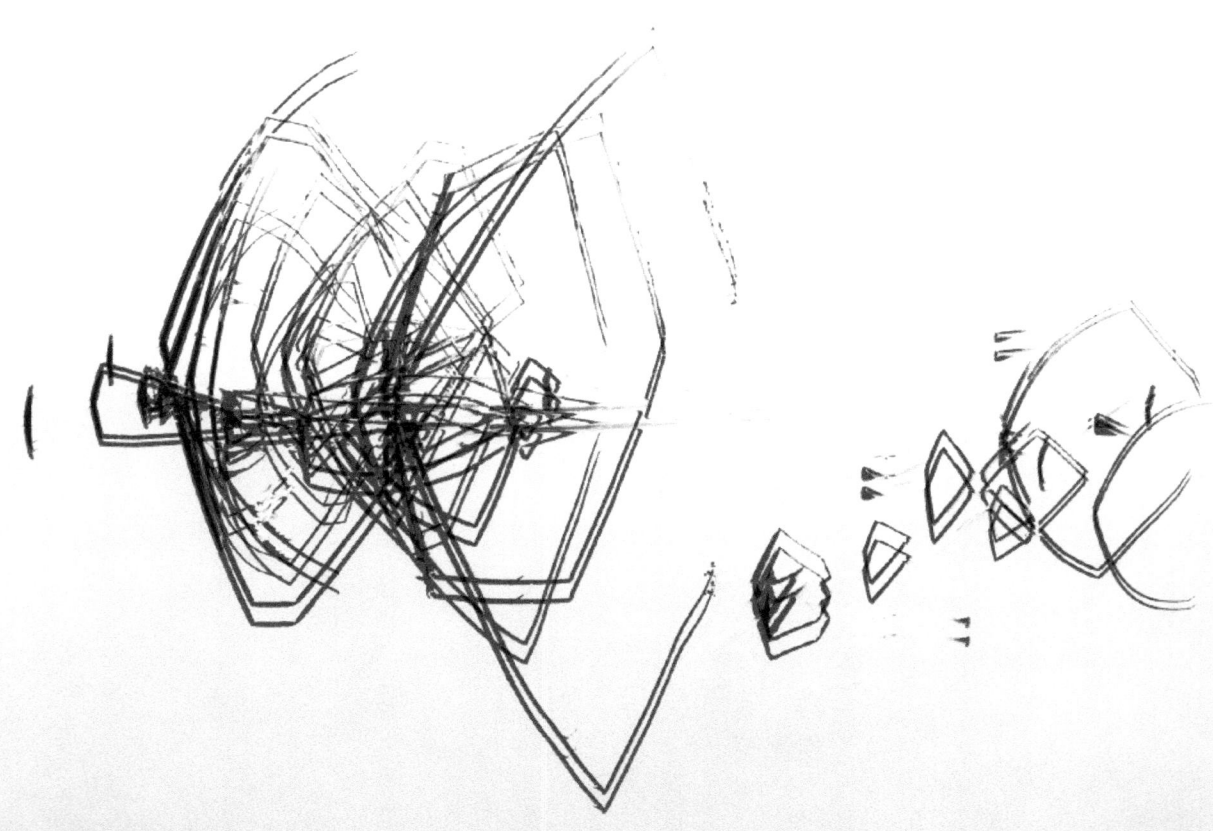

It's not about right or
wrong; you can learn
from anything:
What matters is where
you position yourself
when you look at or
create something.

It is a joy to know that
I have offered you
something.

Thank you for this joy!

www.ingramcontent.com/pod-product-compliance
Lightning Source LLC
Chambersburg PA
CBHW051921210526
45473CB00006B/2093